P9-DGV-410

# THE FLOWERING OF THE THIRD AMERICA

*The Making of an Organizational Society, 1850–1920*

## Maury Klein

*The American Ways Series*

IVAN R. DEE  *Chicago*

*For Priscilla Long*
*Writer, colleague, and the best kind of friend*

THE FLOWERING OF THE THIRD AMERICA. Copyright ©
1993 by Maury Klein. All rights reserved, including the right to
reproduce this book or portions thereof in any form. For
information, address: Ivan R. Dee, Inc., 1332 North Halsted Street,
Chicago 60622. Manufactured in the United States of America and
printed on acid-free paper.

Library of Congress Cataloging-in-Publication Data:
Klein, Maury, 1939–
    The flowering of the third America : the making of an
organizational society, 1850–1920 / Maury Klein.
        p.    cm. — (The American ways series)
    Includes bibliographical references and index.
    ISBN 1-56663-029-0 (cloth : acid-free paper). — ISBN
1-56663-030-4 (pbk. : acid-free paper)
        1. United States—Social conditions—1865–1918.   2. United
States—Economic conditions—1865–1918.   3. Corporate culture—
United States—History.   I. Title.   II. Series.
HN57.K55   1993
306'.0973'09034—dc20                                    93-13869

# The Flowering of the
# Third America

# Contents

Wealth produced by industrial growth is unequally distributed. Massive immigration creates a society of greater diversity than ever before—but more fragmented by organization.

# The Flowering of the
# Third America

# Prologue: The United States in 1850

O beautiful, for spacious skies,
    For amber waves of grain,
For purple mountain majesties
    Above the fruited plain!
America! America!
    God shed His grace on thee
And crown thy good with brotherhood
    From sea to shining sea!

THESE IMMORTAL WORDS were written by a Massachusetts
professor and writer named Katharine Lee Bates in 1893,
after she had been moved by the breathtaking view from
atop Pike's Peak in Colorado. The vision that inspired her
near the century's end belonged to a very different nation
than the one into which she had been born in 1855.

Not until 1850 did the United States actually stretch its
borders from sea to shining sea by making California a
state. Before then the amber waves of grain and fruited
plains all lay east of the Mississippi River, and the purple
mountain majesties floated in a remote and mysterious West
inhabited only by Indians, trappers, miners, soldiers, some
hardy adventurers, and a thriving colony of Mormons.
Many a school atlas still referred to the region as the "Great
American Desert." Iowa, Missouri, Arkansas, Louisiana,
and Texas were the only states west of the Mississippi, and
Texas the only one not directly on the river. Most of the
West had not yet even been organized into territories; much
of it had just come into American hands thanks to the
Mexican War.

In 1850 America was a long way from being crowned with brotherhood. The country still quarreled violently over the presence of slavery and had scarcely begun to grapple with its alter ego, racism, or the prejudice aimed at immigrants from distant lands who would grow steadily more varied and "foreign" in their cultures and customs.

The nation was still younger than its elder citizens, many of whom remembered the Revolution and the Founding Fathers. They had watched proudly as their brash young country wrenched chunks of the continent free from European and Mexican hands and attached them to the stars and stripes. By 1850, however, a dark, brooding sorrow stained this sense of pride. Patriotism still burned strong in the hearts of most citizens, but not as strong in some as the doctrine of secession. The bloody climax of that shifting loyalty still lay eleven years in the future.

The United States of 1850 contained 23.2 million people spread throughout thirty-one states including newcomer California. About 85 percent of them lived on farms or in small villages; the entire country had only 236 towns or cities with 2,500 or more people, and only one city with a population of more than a hundred thousand. Nearly two-thirds of the nation's gainful workers worked on farms, the average size of which was around 203 acres. They toiled with muscle and animal power, having precious little in the way of farm machinery to ease their labor. About 71 percent of all the horsepower produced in the United States in 1850 came from humans or animals.

In this nation of farmers, plantation dwellers, and villagers scattered across a huge continent, less than eight people inhabited an average square mile of land. The distances that separated them went beyond mere miles, but the mileage was formidable enough. The railroad had made a deep impression on American life but still offered only regional travel; the entire nation boasted only 9,021 miles of track. In 1850 a person in New York City could not even reach Albany or Boston by rail, let alone points west. One couple in 1853 spent more than two weeks making their way from Bath, Maine, to Peoria, Illinois.

Longer trips were even more harrowing. A trip from New York to San Francisco by sea took thirty-five days cover 5,250 miles if the traveler risked crossing the malaria-infested Isthmus of Panama, or five months to sail 13,300 miles around dangerous Cape Horn. An overland stage from St. Louis to San Francisco took thirty days to cover 2,800 dangerous and bone-rattling miles. Despite the hardships, eager gold-seekers and others flocked to San Francisco; some 36,462 of them arrived by sea alone in 1850, and thousands more braved the overland trek.

The telegraph too was in its infancy, its frail wires and crude instruments bearing the seeds of a communications revolution. Only about twelve thousand miles of wire had been strung by 1850, leaving the vast majority of people to rely on the time-honored sources of travelers, letters, and newspapers for news of the world beyond their village or farm. Newspapers did not yet draw their news from telegraphic dispatches. Most of the nation's 254 papers were local journals which copied articles from big-city dailies when possible. News of the larger world traveled slowly or not at all to places outside the major cities.

Government at all levels was a small and faint presence. The federal government barely intruded on the lives of most people. Most citizens knew it personally through one of its 18,417 post offices. No other federal agency—the military, the customs service, the mint—touched their lives directly. Federal workers numbered only 26,274, most of them in the postal service, and the military on active duty only 20,824. The federal budget outlay for 1850 totaled only $39.5 million, and interest on the national debt of $63.5 million required only $2.85 from each citizen. Very few Americans ever saw the nation's capital or a real president in the flesh, but most people took their political duties seriously: nearly 73 percent of eligible voters cast ballots in the presidential election of 1848.

In 1850, then, most Americans lived in a world that was overwhelmingly rural with small extremes of wealth or poverty, little ethnic diversity, and a labor force that in half the states still relied on slaves. Life was above all else local, and so were loyalties. Men and women considered themselves Virginians or Pennsylvanians first and then an American because Virginia or Pennsylvania was the tangible world that surrounded their daily life and the one to which their family and friends belonged.

Life in 1850 was far simpler and more elemental than it is today. People moved more slowly and tuned their lives to the rhythms not of the clock but of the sun and the season. They lived closer to nature, if only because those who wrested their living from the land had to struggle daily with the elements. To them nature was not scenery to view or explore; it was both opportunity and enemy, rewarding and punishing their efforts with fickle indifference. Trees were something not to admire but to chop down laboriously to clear fields for planting and provide wood for homes, barns, and fences. Driven by ambition and sometimes desperation, they fought the land, weather, insects, animals, Indians, or anything else that stood in the way of their hopes for a better life. Whatever scars they left in their wake seemed to them trivial; there was so much land and so few people.

Daily life lacked all of our modern conveniences. Indoor plumbing was unknown. People used an outhouse or chamber pot for a toilet, and all water had to be hauled into the house by the family or servants. People bathed less often, and the entire family often used the same bath water because of the work required to fill and empty the large tin tub. Heat came from the fireplace, where cooking was also done unless the family could afford a stove. Both fireplace and stove had to be fed with a constant supply of wood chopped and split. Most people rose with the sun and went to bed with it because they had only candles to provide light. They grew or raised or hunted most of the food they ate and made most of the clothes they wore. Even in cities, where store-bought things could be found, the food was local and of the season.

These conditions made people feel more keenly the elemental differences between warmth and cold, light and darkness, pain and pleasure. For the vast majority who lived outside a town, noise was itself an event. In the quiet of the countryside every sound had a meaning, and none went unnoticed. Country dwellers knew silence as we cannot, and relished simple things in a way we cannot. Pleasure and amusement was for them as simple and homemade as their clothes, except among the well-to-do. A trip was not merely travel but a journey to be described in loving detail to friends and family; a social call or meeting or Sunday at church was an event elevated to a ritual to separate it from the routine of everyday work.

Work and chores occupied most of people's time. Nearly all of it was manual labor. Most men worked for themselves. Few jobs or professions were specialized; men entered them with little preparation and did not hesitate to change careers or do several things at once until they hit on one that suited them. The desire to improve their lot—and the availability of cheap, abundant land—led Americans to move far more often than other people, but the places they lived and the patterns of their lives did not vary much. If they did well and acquired some property, they could improve their social

nding and in that way change their lives. This was the
pe, the dream, of most people, the spur that drove them to
re work or yet another move.

Family and religion remained the twin pillars of the social
er, the source of education, moral instruction, and enter-
ment. In 1850 only about 59 percent of boys and 33
cent of girls were enrolled in schools. These numbers
uded only whites; the figure for blacks, most of whom
e slaves, was a paltry 1.8 percent.

People also lived closer to death in an age when medical
and scientific knowledge were still primitive. Death often
came suddenly and without warning. Diseases of all kinds
cut people down from infancy on, and the cures prescribed
by doctors often did more harm than good. The federal
government kept no statistics on such things in those days,
and Massachusetts was virtually alone in trying to gather
information. In that state a male baby born in 1850 could
expect to live only 38.3 years, a girl 40.5 years; more than 13
percent of infants died at birth. Everywhere tuberculosis, the
"white death," was a major killer, and periodic scourges of
diphtheria, scarlet fever, cholera, and other diseases ravaged
villages and farms no less than cities. The entire nation had
only fifty-two medical schools and two dental schools. In
1850 the latter graduated a grand total of seventeen new
practitioners.

This close relationship with death helps explain why
religion was so important to most Americans. Whatever the
creed or church, religion eased the pain of suffering and loss
and prepared one's mind for whatever calamity might strike.
In this elemental world most Americans steered their lives
by basic values simply put and fiercely held: love of God,
country, and family. People might stray far from these tenets
in practice, but they clutched the beliefs fiercely and returned to them in times of trial.

Young and brash as the country was in 1850, it was already fashioning a culture as varied as its landscape and the people who inhabited it. The year saw the arrival of a new publication called *Harper's Monthly Magazine*, which soon became a major voice on the literary and political scene. A bright young man named Mathew Brady heralded the advent of a wondrous new technology called photography by publishing a book of his portraits. Nathaniel Hawthorne gave the nation a brilliant if daring new novel called *The Scarlet Letter*, while composer Stephen Foster contributed a new song called "Camptown Races." Jenny Lind, the "Swedish Nightingale" and the best-known singer in the world, toured the United States under the management of a shrewd impresario named P. T. Barnum. A bold woman named Mrs. Amelia Jenks Bloomer unveiled to a startled public the peculiar trouserlike piece of clothing for women that came to bear her name.

A loud sigh of relief went up across the nation when the Compromise of 1850 seemingly put to rest the long and acrid fight over slavery and expansion. Although there were grumblings north and south over the terms, most people hoped that these cancerous issues had been laid to rest for good. A treaty with Great Britain that same year appeared to remove growing tensions over who had what rights to build a canal across the Isthmus of Panama. For the moment peace beckoned, and with it a prosperity that had eluded the nation during the depression-racked 1840s.

This portrait of the United States in 1850 is a still life of a preindustrial society on the brink of becoming an industrial one. A person born that year would reach the ripe age of seventy in 1920. Katharine Lee Bates, author of the words to "America," spanned this era: she was born in 1855 and lived until 1929. Those who belonged to her generation had the unique privilege of witnessing the dawn of the modern world. The structure of every aspect of society, and the details of everyday life, changed more in those seventy years than in all the centuries of recorded history before them.

This book is the story of the forces that made it possible to change so decisively not only the material world but the course of human destiny in the span of a single lifetime.

# 1

# The Industrializing of America

The last half century has written the most brilliant records ever given...to the annals of the world's history, in every attribute of civilized advancement. Progress has been unexampled in art, in science, in industry, in commerce, in finance and trade, as well as in achievement in field and forum. The great republic of the new world has vastly outstripped the progress of any other half century or indeed, of any full century since the world was.

—Alexander K. McClure,
*Recollections of Half a Century* (1902)

THIS EXTRAVAGANT BOAST by a Pennsylvania politico said what many Americans felt about their nation at the turn of the century. Whatever their problems or shortcomings as a people, Americans had forged a material civilization unlike any other in history, unmatched in the wealth it piled up and the scale on which that wealth was distributed. The way in which this was done lies near the heart of our great national myth, known loosely as the American Dream, wherein poor but ambitious newcomers to the country seize the opportunities offered them and, through hard work, sacrifice, and struggle, improve their lot and in some cases make the fabled journey from rags to riches.

To these seekers of a better life America was the land of

opportunity precisely because it had so much land available. Throughout history land had always been the primary source of wealth, and America offered more fertile land than any place on the globe. More important, it possessed a political and social system that encouraged newcomers to start life anew in a new world. From this unique condition emerged a central paradox of American life: despite the steady flow of immigrants in colonial times and later, there was always far more land than there were people to work it. To solve that problem the settlers turned to two solutions that profoundly shaped the destiny of the country: slavery and technology.

Slavery left in its wake not only a bloody civil war but two centuries of racial turmoil that have not yet ceased. Technology, by contrast, became the engine of progress on which the United States rode to prosperity and greatness. It rendered slavery obsolete as a labor system but could not touch the larger, more sensitive issue of slavery as a form of racial control. The revolution in technology came too late to spare the nation the horrors and legacy of slavery, but it did work a miracle of another kind: technology transformed the economy into one in which land ceased to be the dominant form of wealth.

Industrialization created this miracle and for that reason remains the great divide of American (and indeed world) history, shaping a society so unlike the one that had gone before as to be unrecognizable. Industrialization transcended ideologies, defied political strictures, ignored moral dictums, overturned social orders, and unraveled the fabric of tradition. It became a revolutionary force by solving the oldest problem of humanity: scarcity. Since the dawn of time people had struggled to obtain the essentials of life: food, water, clothing, shelter, heat, protection from enemies. None of the great civilizations that arose and flourished over the centuries succeeded in solving this problem.

It was in fact two problems: one of production (how to create goods faster than the population grew), the other of distribution (how to apportion goods among members of a society). During the preindustrial era scarcity remained a way of life for most people because productivity was too low to raise the overall standard of living, and goods were distributed unevenly, which meant that a privileged few enjoyed most of them. The discovery of the New World excited people because it offered an escape from the shackles of scarcity. It had a mind-boggling abundance of everything the Old World lacked: land, resources, water, wood, and freedom. Even better, these things existed in pristine form, unshackled by social and political systems. The promise of America was not just its staggering array of resources but its *potential* for creating wealth.

Industrialization realized that potential on a scale never before possible. By solving the problem of scarcity, it laid the foundation for a new era in human society in which scarcity became more a problem of distribution than of production. The process by which this occurred involved a number of factors deeply enmeshed with one another. The most important of these factors for the American industrial experience are:

1. Power-driven machinery replaced human and animal muscle as a source of energy.

2. Technological innovations penetrated every area of economic activity and greatly increased productivity.

3. Production came to be centered in factories or other centrally located facilities.

4. A transportation revolution speeded the flow of goods and people.

5. A communications revolution speeded the flow of information.

6. A full-blown market economy extended its reach beyond the local level to regional and national levels.

7. An organizational revolution restructured American business enterprise and ultimately the whole society.

8. Specialization began to characterize every aspect of economic activity.

9. Population increased at unprecedented rates.

10. The number of cities and towns, and the proportion of Americans living in them, increased sharply.

It is important to view these items not as "causes" of industrialization but as factors interacting with one another continually over time to create a dynamic process of change. They are sources rather than causes, and influenced one another in ways that made them inseparable. Some of them will be discussed here, the rest in later chapters.

Advances in technology were central to the industrial experience. The myth of Americans as inventive, mechanical geniuses with a love for gadgets goes back to the preindustrial era when there was so much work to be done and so few people to do it. A machine is simply a device with interrelated parts that function together to perform some kind of work. One early example reveals how simple devices could profoundly alter the future. The cotton gin, invented by Eli Whitney in 1793, solved the problem of removing seed from cotton so easily and cheaply that it allowed cotton to become the major staple crop of the South. The spread of cotton in turn fostered the growth of slavery and fastened the system ever tighter upon Southern culture.

Other new machines followed the example of the cotton gin in performing with ease tasks that had once been laborious and time consuming. The textile industry was the first to be transformed as a host of new devices allowed the work to be centralized in large establishments called mills. By 1815 the country had 213 textile mills, most of them in New England where water power was plentiful.

Machines spread quickly to the farm, where they were most urgently needed. As early as 1795 an ingenious Delaware farmer named Oliver Evans created a continuous-process flour mill that cut the labor needed in half. The first cast-iron plow was patented in 1797, followed two years later by a seeding machine. The first reapers appeared in the early 1830s, the first crude thresher 1837–1840, and the first steel plow in 1837. Other inventions followed in rapid order: the revolving disc harrow (1847), binder (1850), twine knotter (1858), and checkrower corn planter (1864), along with improved versions of older machines.

"It is truly a sublime sight," gushed a writer in *Scientific American* in the late nineteenth century, "to behold a machine performing nearly all the functions of a rational being." A swelling stream of new inventions poured forth from the workshops of American tinkerers even before the Civil War. The average number of patents granted each year leaped from six hundred in the 1830s to almost five thousand by 1860. While most of these vanished into oblivion, the survivors included such innovations as the revolver, sewing machine, rotary printing press, shoe manufacturing machines, locks, vulcanized rubber, food canning, power tools, and the first crude electric motors.

Not surprisingly, building machine tools became an industry at which Americans excelled. The first screw-cutting machine appeared in 1809, the circular saw in 1814, and the profile lathe in 1818. The Brown and Sharpe Company of Providence, Rhode Island, produced the first commercial vernier caliper in 1851 and soon developed a wide reputation for its precision tools, instruments, and clocks. As industrialization proceeded, the metals and machinery sector grew steadily in importance. But before 1830, as business historian Alfred D. Chandler, Jr., notes, American machines tended to be small, flimsy, and made of wood. Something more was needed to thrust them into a pivotal position in the production process.

Industrialization lacked two key ingredients for rapid expansion: fuel and iron, in cheap, reliable sources. In 1830 nearly all American machines relied on water power because other forms of energy were too scarce or expensive. The forests that seemed so inexhaustible to the early settlers were depleted at a startling rate, especially in the East. Coal was available, but the Northeast had to import it from Virginia or England. The opening of the enormous Pennsylvania anthracite coal fields in the 1830s touched off an explosion of economic growth. In 1825 less than 389,000 tons of coal were mined from these fields; by 1849 the yield exceeded 3.8 million tons.

Anthracite provided cheap, clean fuel for a region where nearly all the machines and mills had to rely on water power or imported coal for energy. The textile mills of southern New England lacked the water power to compete successfully with their northern rivals, but in 1828 Samuel Slater opened a new era by erecting the first integrated steam textile mill in Providence. New and larger mills could be built in coastal areas lacking water power, and often at cheaper cost because they did not need to install complicated hydraulic systems.

Cheap coal also transformed the iron industry, so vital to an expanding industrial economy. Originally it consisted of small, scattered works that relied on water-driven forges to produce iron for village blacksmiths who shaped it into tools, wire, spikes, hoes, rakes, shovels, axes, horseshoes, plows, stoves, kettles, and other products. The rapid growth of iron production led to a separation of the mining of iron ore from its processing. Anthracite, with its lower cost, much higher heat, and fewer impurities, led to the introduction of such new techniques as the hot blast furnace (1840) and the Bessemer process for converting pig iron into steel (1850s). Americans borrowed two innovations from the British: the rolling mill, a machine that cut the labor needed to refine and shape iron into bars, and the puddling process, which enabled iron manufacturers to use coal for fuel and produce on a greater scale.

Coal also became a primary fuel for the most crucial machine of the industrial age, the locomotive. Machines had been around long before the Industrial Revolution, but they were always limited in their use by the source of power, which had to be human or animal muscle or nature (usually water).

Here too, technology transformed habits that were centuries old into a stunning new array of possibilities. The development of the steam engine between 1706 and 1782 culminated in James Watt's rotary engine, which radically transformed a host of industries. Steam power was introduced into sawmills in 1798, but its influence was felt most powerfully in textiles, iron-making, and mining.

Without the steam engine and cheap fuel to run it, the factory system would not have spread far from New England. The word is shorthand for "manufactory," which as late as 1812 consisted overwhelmingly of goods made in the home for family use. In the preindustrial world production took place in simple forms on a small scale. Craftsmen, working at home, produced goods on order for merchants who furnished raw materials to people working at home, collected piecework from them, and had the pieces assembled in a central shop. This "putting-out" system was used for woven cloth, shoes, hats, and other products. Even mining and iron manufacturing were done by small, local firms located near the raw material and sources of water for power.

The advent of machinery changed every aspect of this production process. Machines were expensive, immobile, and had to be located near a source of power. To be profitable they had to produce in quantity, which required a steady supply of raw materials, a reliable labor force, some kind of quality control, accounting procedures to keep track of everything, access to markets, and enough capital to keep the business going. In short, the production process had to be centralized in one place where its operation could be carefully organized and managed.

The result was a new kind of institution known as the factory, which revolutionized labor relations no less than production methods. It brought together in one place a permanent work force; paid them a fixed daily wage that was their only source of income; compelled them to work specific hours and thus to order their lives around that schedule; gave them routinized, specialized tasks to perform instead of a whole product to make; and created a new class known as managers or supervisors to oversee their work, thereby separating them from contact with the owners of the company.

The Boston Manufacturing Company at Waltham pioneered this process and became the model for the American factory system. Using a labor force of three hundred to tend its machines, the textile mill mechanized production as much as possible, integrated the spinning and weaving processes, operated its own machine shops to keep the machinery in repair, and sold all its goods through one agent to keep costs low. To get workers, the company recruited young women from New England farms and housed them in special dormitories near the plant.

The key to the Boston system was precisely that it was a

system—coordinated, integrated, and standardized to produce a single item (cheap coarse cotton fabrics) for a
growing market. The availability of cheap coal allowed the
factory system to spread quickly into glass, paper, sugar
refining, and other industries. Cheap, plentiful iron supplies
revitalized the metals industries. As early as the 1790s Eli
Whitney—the same man who gave the world the cotton
gin—had used a government contract for muskets to introduce a new principle of production based on using precision-
made, interchangeable parts put together by semiskilled
workmen in large quantity on a routine basis.

Whitney put into practice the virtue of division of labor
extolled by the great economist Adam Smith. While others
used power-driven machinery to fabricate simple wares,
Whitney applied machines to the creation of more intricate
mechanisms. His "uniformity system" replaced the slow,
careful labor of craftsmen with the precision of machines
making parts quickly and cheaply. The workers were slow
to grasp this novel idea. "They are as good as any workmen," Whitney sighed, "but I cannot make them understand
how I would have a thing done till it is Done." The key to
his approach, as biographer Constance Green observes, was
"his execution of a carefully-thought-out system, of which
every separate type of machine was a part."

Whitney's experiment illustrated several of the basic factors of the industrialization process at work in one operation. To produce firearms in quantity he built a factory that
relied on power-driven machinery. By breaking the production process down into simple tasks and specializing the
function of each worker, he could use an inexperienced labor
force to build complex machines. Nor did Whitney stop
there. In 1818 he gave the industrial world another pivotal
invention, the milling machine, which could cut and shape
metal parts with far greater precision and speed than any-

ing done by hand. "In some respects," declared Constance
reen, "the man who invented the miller in 1818 was a
eater benefactor to his country than the inventor of the
tton gin itself." Whitney's miller soon became (and re-
ains) standard equipment in any shop where intricate and
ecise metal parts were needed.

The most far-reaching influence of machines driven by
am power came in the field of transportation. The first
successful steamboat in 1807 revolutionized water travel by
enabling river boats to go upstream for the first time and by
freeing oceangoing ships from dependence on the wind.
Even this achievement paled before the influence of steam
power on land travel. John Stevens, who invented the first
screw propeller for boats in 1802, devised the first locomotive with a multitubular boiler in 1826. Four years later
Peter Cooper built the first American locomotive and set in
motion a revolution in inland transportation that reshaped
not only travel and shipping but the whole fabric of American life.

The transportation revolution was already under way
when the railroad appeared on the scene. On this vast
continent distance was always the great barrier to settlement,
and it did little good to increase productivity without some
way to get goods to markets. By 1815 improved roads, new
bridges, and growing use of riverboats were already driving
down the cost of transportation. During the next twenty
years huge sums of money were poured into constructing
turnpikes and canals. Completion of the 362-mile Erie Canal
in 1825 connected Lake Erie to the Hudson River, enabling
boats to reach New York City and the ocean. By far the
longest canal in the world, the Erie attracted so much traffic
that it had to be enlarged only ten years later. Between 1816
and 1840 enthusiastic Americans spent $125 million to
construct 3,226 miles of canals. Three of these new canals

gave Pennsylvania anthracite access to eastern markets; nevertheless, most canals failed to repay the investment.

Water shipping dominated American transportation well past the Civil War, thanks to the nation's impressive river system, but it had serious drawbacks. Boats could go only where there were navigable waterways, and were shut out of whole regions during the winter months when the water froze. They moved slowly and had to follow the endless meanderings of rivers filled with snags, sandbars, and other obstructions. Railroads solved all these problems. They could go almost anywhere in a straighter line at faster speeds through nearly any kind of weather all year long. They could run on regular schedules and fit their equipment to customer needs.

The frenzy of optimism that had earlier seized on canals quickly transferred to the laying of rails. By 1860 the nation boasted 30,626 miles of track, and the flow of grain from the Midwestern states had begun to shift from its north-south axis down the Mississippi River to an overland east-west rail route. After the war the railroad mania raged so furiously that by 1900 the nation had 193,246 miles of rail, more than the rest of the world combined. This elaborate network proved crucial in the growth of the American industrial economy.

Railroads opened new markets and developed old ones by giving them connections to new outlets. They hastened the settlement of whole regions of the country, especially west of the Mississippi River where distance was a major obstacle. Farmers, cattlemen, merchants, businessmen of all kinds, immigrants, and others flocked west to carve a new future for themselves, creating new towns where none had existed and turning sleepy villages into booming commercial centers. While the railroad turned ambitious cities into large metropolises, its deepest influence was felt in small, remote towns.

"The railroads," noted historian Albro Martin, "made small-town America." They removed much of the isolation that was so large a part of life on a vast continent, enabling people to reach nearby towns or distant cities with an ease never before known. Railroads also brought the outside world to the town in the form of goods, salesmen, settlers, touring performers, and visitors. In the West the rapidly spreading rail network literally created towns where none had existed before and connected them to other places on the national map.

But the railroad's significance extended far beyond its immediate effects. By regularizing the shipment of goods and people, trains routinized transportation as no other form ever had. By lowering the cost of shipping, they rendered distant markets not only accessible but economically feasible. In less than a single lifetime the rail system became the lifeline of industrial America. Moreover, the explosive growth of railroads made them a leading consumer of such products as iron and steel, coal, lumber, and heavy machinery. A host of other industries, most notably iron and steel, owed their growth to the railroads' voracious appetite for equipment and supplies.

As the nation's first big business, the railroads provided a model for large corporations doing business over an entire region. They pioneered in new methods of finance, accounting, and organization, and were the first corporations to raise large amounts of capital in public markets. The early stock and bond exchanges consisted overwhelmingly of railroad securities. The railroads were also the first industry to handle a large and scattered labor force, to confront the problems of competition on a large scale, and to be regulated by state and federal governments. In all these roles they set precedents that were followed, for better or worse, by giant industrial corporations.

The transportation revolution did much to open up regional and national markets, but it could not have gone far without a parallel breakthrough in communications. As the nation expanded, the flow of business grew ever more dependent on the flow of information. Before 1840 news moved in the same ways it had since antiquity: a message could travel no faster than the messenger who carried it. Then a stunning new technology revolutionized the flow of information by transmitting it almost instantly.

The magnetic telegraph launched the age of media. Largely the brainchild of Samuel F. B. Morse, who gave his first public demonstration in 1844, the telegraph spread with lightning speed throughout the nation after a fumbling start. Gradually a number of smaller telegraph companies were gobbled up by a firm called Western Union, which by 1870 handled almost 9.2 million messages in 3,972 offices connected by 112,000 miles of wire. Like railroad mileage, these figures grew by astounding leaps until by 1900 they totaled more than 63 million messages, 22,900 offices, and 933,000 miles of wire.

Once the telegraph gained acceptance, it set a pattern for later innovations in communications by moving swiftly from a novelty to a necessity of daily life. Railroad companies overcame early doubts to form a symbiotic relationship with the telegraph. Wires were strung along railroad rights-of-way, and offices were installed in rail depots where operators served both the public and the railroad. Telegraph dispatches made travel faster and safer by regulating the movement of trains heading in both directions on a single track.

Newspapers grasped the potential of the telegraph early and used it to gather stories from around the country. By the 1850s "telegraphic dispatches" had become a prominent feature in most major newspapers and had already begun to influence politics and public opinion. During the secession crisis in the fall of 1860, President James Buchanan protested that "The public mind throughout the interior is kept in a constant state of excitement by what are called 'telegrams.' They are short and spicy, and can easily be inserted in the country journals. In the city journals they can be contradicted the next day; but the case is different throughout the country."

The new "lightning wire" also changed the way bankers, brokers, merchants, and speculators did business. Fast access to information from across the nation led to the rise of Wall Street as the center of financial markets. Other kinds of markets, such as the commodities exchange in Chicago, also centralized their activity in one location, as did companies that conducted operations in several states. The telegraph offered merchants a whole new style of doing business. "Operations are made in *one day* with its aid, by repeated communications," marveled one observer in 1847, "which could not be done in from two to four weeks by mail." This sense of wonder reached new heights later in the century with the advent of another technological breakthrough, the telephone, which allowed people to speak directly into the "ether."

The interaction among these factors became strikingly clear as the century wore on. The telegraph speeded up rail operations while the growth of the rail network allowed mail to be carried in greater volume to more places at lower cost on specially made postal cars where huge bags of mail were sorted during the trip. By the 1870s the American postal service had already become the largest and most efficient in the world. Thirty years later its 76,688 post offices were handling 7 billion items of mail, nearly twice their load of 1886. Postal contracts with railroads enabled

Congress to establish rural free delivery in 1896, which in turn permitted the rise of a new retailing industry through catalogs. Two companies in particular, Montgomery Ward and Sears, Roebuck, created giant enterprises by tapping the mail-order market.

The transportation and communications revolutions spurred settlement across this far-flung nation and with it the rise of regional and national markets. Market is a word that often confuses people because it has several meanings. In simplest terms it is a place for exchanging goods for money or other goods, but the word is also used as an abstraction to describe all persons or firms engaged in transactions over some particular item such as stocks or wheat or land. These buyers and sellers seldom meet directly but conduct their business through agents called brokers.

Markets serve the crucial function of determining price levels for commodities through the process of buying and selling. A subsistence economy, in which people produce only for their own use, has no need of a market, but once people begin to sell their surplus goods or produce solely for sale, some mechanism is necessary to determine prices. Since markets tend to proliferate as the economy grows more complex, the growth of a market system has long been linked to the process of economic development. Economist Karl Polanyi considered it to be the central feature of the Industrial Revolution. In his description, notice how he relates several of our factors:

> But how shall this revolution be defined? ... all these [developments] were incidental to one basic change, the establishment of market economy.... The nature of this institution cannot be fully grasped unless the impact of the machine on a commercial society is fully realized. We do not intend to assert that the machine caused what

happened, but we insist that once elaborate machines and plant were used for production in a commercial society, the idea of a self-regulating market was bound to take shape.

In a preindustrial society, agriculture dominates economic activity. Much of the commerce involves agricultural goods, and those who make nonfarm goods produce in small quantities and sell to local markets. Once machinery enters the process, however, it changes everything radically. Since producing with machines is expensive, it becomes feasible only if goods can be produced in quantity and an assured flow of raw materials can be obtained. Meeting these conditions requires a whole new framework of economic activity in which every aspect is reduced to a market transaction. Polanyi described it this way:

> The transformation implies a change in the motive of action on the part of every member of society: for the motive of subsistence that of gain must be substituted. All transactions are turned into money transactions.... All incomes must derive from the sale of something or other, and whatever the actual source of a person's income, it must be regarded as resulting from sale. No less is implied in the simple term "market system," by which we designate the institutional pattern described.

As the number and size of markets increase, they become more interconnected as well. Gradually, as the industrial economy matures, these once isolated markets coalesce into a full-blown market economy, or what Polanyi called the "One Big Market." Once established, the market economy tends to become self-adjusting or self-regulating. Prices regulate themselves, and profits are at the mercy of market fluctuations. All economic elements are converted into commodities and find their own price level within the system: goods are sold at commodity prices, services for salary or commission, labor for wages, land for rent, money for interest.

Something else happens as well: the noneconomic aspects of every factor come to be overshadowed by their new market role as mere commodities to be bought and sold. Gradually the market economy nudges into being a market society subordinate to its needs. Of course, markets and prices are never fully self-regulating; they can be distorted by creating artificial surplus or scarcity, or most typically by government policy. It is in the area of government policy that the American experience deviates sharply from that of most other nations.

The American economic system was shaped by the same ideals that underlay its political creed: freedom and liberty. Americans embraced the notion of self-regulating markets and government noninterference so fervently that by the early nineteenth century "free enterprise" or "laissez-faire" principles were infiltrating our economic system. The self-regulating market economy squared neatly with the beliefs of a people who worshiped freedom from restraint, individual liberty, economic opportunity, and rugged individualism. Underwritten by law and by the courts, which usually ruled against government restriction or regulation, the American economy in the nineteenth century was probably the most open system that has ever existed.

Here, then, was a vast continent teeming with resources and a growing population eager to exploit them in an economic and political framework that maximized their liberty to seize opportunities without restraints. A more perfect hothouse for economic growth could hardly have been designed. The result was nothing less than an economic miracle, but it did not occur evenly. The explosive economic growth of the century after 1830 came in bursts, as one might expect from an unregulated system. It was a process of accretion in which gains built upon each other through interaction among the factors listed earlier.

During the 1830s the spread of anthracite coal into Eastern markets helped spur the transformation of the iron industry and the development of the railroad system. By the 1840s the rail and telegraph systems were expanding rapidly along with the factory system. All three made unprecedented strides in the 1850s, which saw huge gains in agricultural crops, railroad and telegraph mileage, large factories, and a host of new inventions including the sewing machine, harvester, and breech-loading firearm.

Between 1839 and 1899 total commodity output in the United States increased elevenfold, or almost 50 percent every decade. Since the population grew at less than half this rate, the output per capita in 1899 was two and a half times that of 1839. No other country in the world could match this rate of growth over so extended a period. The United States was already a wealthy country before 1840; in the decades ahead it surged to a position as the leading material civilization in the world.

# 2

# The New Entrepreneurs

> The organization of the American economy, since its
> beginning, has been centered around the contribu-
> tion of the individual following his own interests
> and motives.... There are no "forces of history,"
> only human action, and the human beings involved
> are individuals as well as parts of society. Men make
> economic change.
>
> —Jonathan R. T. Hughes,
> *The Vital Few* (1966)

THEY HAVE BEEN called everything from "Captains
of Industry" to "Robber Barons," from "Masters of Capital"
to "Lords of Creation." They are the entrepreneurs who
oversaw and in many ways created the transformation of the
American economy into a juggernaut of wealth and productivity. The names of the most famous among them are
familiar to most Americans: Vanderbilt, Rockefeller, Carnegie, Gould, Harriman, Morgan, Swift. To this day they
remain controversial because we have never quite decided
whether to admire what they did more than despise how
they did it. Our mixed reaction to these men reveals much
about our values as a people and our attitude toward the
influences that shaped our modern world.

The dictionary defines an entrepreneur as a person who
organizes and manages an enterprise. But he is no ordinary

manager or organizer. Back in 1800 French economist Jean Baptiste Say defined him as one who "shifts economic resources out of an area of lower and into an area of higher productivity and greater yield." The entrepreneur thrives on seizing opportunities that are unnoticed or ignored by others to produce something new or something old in a new way. He is, above all, an innovator. As management expert Peter Drucker has observed, "Innovation is the specific tool of entrepreneurs, the means by which they exploit change as an opportunity for a different business or a different service."

As an innovator bringing change into a static situation, the entrepreneur upsets the usual way of doing things. His gain will often be someone else's loss as the new product or service elbows aside older, less efficient rivals. Joseph Schumpeter, who paid more attention to entrepreneurs than any other economist, called the capitalistic process itself one of creative destruction, "incessantly revolutionizing the economic structure from within, incessantly destroying the old one, incessantly erecting a new one." In this process the entrepreneur became the primary agent of change.

The entrepreneur can also be viewed as a kind of artist who works in another medium for expressing human creativity. He shares with other creative artists the same mixture of desirable and unpalatable traits: vision, genius, ambition, determination, drive, and ruthlessness. "The typical entrepreneur," notes Schumpeter, "is more self-centered than other types, because he relies less than they do on tradition and connection and because his characteristic task . . . consists precisely in breaking up old, and creating new, tradition."

It is important to remember, however, that innovation is different from invention. Even the great entrepreneurs did not usually invent anything; what they did was create the conditions by which an invention or idea could be realized. Inventions have no economic effect until they are known and used, and the task of transforming any improvement into a practical success is very different from that of inventing it. Since few people possess both talents, the history of an invention usually has two sides to its story: the conceiving and inventing of the object, and the struggle to give it life in the marketplace.

While entrepreneurs can be found throughout history, they naturally flourished when circumstances were most conducive to their efforts. Few times were more favorable than the early industrial era, and nowhere were conditions more ideal than in the United States. American entrepreneurs dared dream huge dreams precisely because they operated in an environment free of fetters. They could think big because opportunity *was* big. The United States in the nineteenth century was a unique spawning bed for opportunity and innovation. The social and political framework had plenty of shortcomings, some of which led to a long and bloody civil war in mid-century, but for purposes of economic development it could hardly have been more ideal.

The reason for this, and indeed for many of the flaws as well, lay in the basic values embedded in American society. The American Dream had at its heart not only the idea of liberty but also of economic betterment for the individual. It was an open system that allowed people to go as far as their talent, drive, and luck took them without the shackles of class or government restraints. How far a person went was usually measured by economic gain, which eventually translated into social status.

This strong material element behind the American Dream explains why the new world became known early as the Land of Opportunity. Hector St. John de Crèvecoeur, a Frenchman who settled in Orange County, New York, described its appeal in the 1770s:

There is room for everybody in America: has he any particular talent, or industry? he exerts it in order to produce a livelihood, and it succeeds. Is he a merchant? the avenues of trade are infinite; is he eminent in any respect? he will be employed and respected. Does he love a country life? pleasant farms present themselves; he may purchase what he wants, and thereby become an American farmer. Is he a labourer, sober and industrious? he need not go many miles...before he will be hired, well fed at the table of his employer, and paid four or five times more than he can get in Europe. Does he want uncultivated lands? thousands of acres present themselves, which he may purchase cheap.

Notice that Crèvecoeur describes not wealth but the potential for wealth. It was a promise, nothing more. To extract it required hard work and the willingness to endure incredible hardships. This struggle wore out several generations of Americans and sent many of them to premature graves while learning the art of survival. It also helps explain why Americans value individualism so highly and refer to their peculiar brand of it as Rugged Individualism. They fought the Revolution in large measure to free themselves from restraints on these values and to take their destiny into their own hands. The promise of America could be realized only with an open system and a government that preserved and extended it.

Government did its part by imposing as few restraints as possible on individual action in the economy. This occurred not by accident but by design. "From about 1800 to 1870," writes legal scholar J. Willard Hurst, "we can see a pattern of surprisingly deliberate and self-conscious policy...that law should increase men's liberty by enlarging their practical range of options in the face of limiting circumstances." American law tried to promote the release of individual creative liberty on as broad a basis as possible by fostering an environment that maximized the range of choices open to people. This approach made law dynamic rather than static, as Hurst explains:

> We were a people going places in a hurry.... We did not devote the prime energies of our legal growth to protecting those who sought the law's shelter simply for what they had; our enthusiasm ran rather to those who wanted the law's help positively to bring things about.... The nineteenth-century United States valued change more than stability and valued stability most often where it helped create a framework for change. The century so highly valued change because imagination could scarcely conceive that it could be other than for the better.

The law did this in several ways. Bankruptcy statutes were framed in such a way as to allow debtors enough breathing space to survive their downfall and get back into the game again. This proved crucial in the turbulent American economy, where many of the most successful entrepreneurs failed one or more times before hitting it big. Other societies shackled debtors so severely that they could do little to repay their obligations, much less try something else. Here laws of tort were construed in ways that defined and limited damage awards so as not to penalize risk-takers.

Nowhere was this aim more obvious than in contract law. A steady expansion of contract law during the period 1800–1875 lifted restrictions on the transfer of land and made it easier to conduct business at a distance. It created new and easier ways for dealing with credit, agency, employment, leases, and other agreements. Gradually the corporation was redefined from an instrument of mercantile policy for serving the state to a potent tool for private development. Later the courts protected private enterprises from attempts by the state to regulate their activities. As Hurst emphasized, "The general extension of contract expressed, above all else, the increasing dominance of the market in social organization."

In these and other ways the law actively promoted and protected an open system that maximized the ability of individuals to pursue their economic interests. To see the difference, one need only look at nineteenth-century Russia, which also had vast lands and resources inviting development. But Russia had a closed system built around an autocratic government, a rigid class structure, and an economic and legal system shackled with restrictions. Far from being rewarded, individual enterprise was stifled, punished, or simply lost in the shuffle.

In the United States, with its ideal climate for nourishing the entrepreneurial spirit, every village had its hustler eager to find the right path to success and fortune. Cities and towns were crowded with them, bumping into one another in their impatience to get ahead. "It would be difficult to describe the avidity with which the American rushes forward to secure this immense booty that fortune offers," wrote that incomparable French observer of American life in the 1830s, Alexis de Tocqueville. He added:

> In the pursuit he fearlessly braves the arrow of the Indian and the diseases of the forest; he is unimpressed by the silence of the woods; the approach of beasts of prey do not disturb him, for he is goaded onwards by a passion stronger than the love of life. Before him lies a boundless continent, and he urges onward as if time pressed and he was afraid of finding no room for his exertions.

In their quest for riches or at least a good living, Americans did not hesitate to change what they did or where they lived. If the land wore out or prospects fizzled out, they packed up and moved somewhere else; if their line of work hit a dead end, they took up something else, maybe two or three something elses. It is impossible even to estimate the number of entrepreneurs because we remember only the most successful ones. In a nation that worships success, we quickly forget that every happy ending was surrounded by a large number of sad ones. Even in the nineteenth century the American landscape was littered with the broken dreams of men whose ideas, large and small, for making their fortune never panned out. The most crowded ghost town in America is the one where the spirits of failed entrepreneurs dwell.

But if success was in short supply, hope and promise never were. Enough men struck it rich to inspire others into more strenuous efforts to follow suit. One generation of Americans in particular had the good luck to appear on the scene at the best possible time for entrepreneurial success. Born between 1830 and 1844, just as industrialization was taking off, this group came of age on the eve of the Civil War. At first glance that might not seem a stroke of good fortune, but these young men followed a course that enabled them to dominate the business world after the war: they chose to avoid military service and concentrate instead on their careers.

Even a sample roster of these men reads like a "Who's Who" of the industrial age: Philip D. Armour, George F. Baker, Andrew Carnegie, A. J. Cassatt, William A. Clark, Charles Deere, Joseph W. Drexel, Marshall Field, Jim Fisk, Jay Gould, Mark Hanna, James J. Hill, August Juilliard, J. P. Morgan, Frederick Pabst, Charles A. Pillsbury, George M. Pullman, John D. and William Rockefeller, H. H. Rogers, Clement Studebaker, Gustavus Swift, Cornelius Vanderbilt III, John Wanamaker, Frederick Weyerhauser, William C. Whitney, Peter Widener, and Charles T. Yerkes. It would be hard to find a comparable list of leading entrepreneurs from any other era, and this roster could be expanded by several times with little effort. Not only is the team strong but the bench is very deep.

Americans have long regarded the Civil War as the dividing line of their history. Whether this is true or not, the war did help create an ideal environment for rapid industrialization and entrepreneurial enterprise. It swept away the bitter political controversies of the antebellum era, especially the corrosive battle over slavery. More important, it crushed the Southern planter class that had dominated national politics for most of the century. When the Southern states seceded in 1860–1861, they abandoned Congress to the control of the rising Republican party, which had an agenda far more inclined to industrial growth than the agricultural interests behind the Democratic party.

The changeover became strikingly clear during the war years as the Republicans passed a flood of legislation that had been blocked for years by Southern congressmen. The Morrill Tariff of 1861 imposed higher rates that benefited such major industries as iron and steel, textiles, paper, glass, and leather. The National Bank Act of 1863 replaced the old Independent Treasury System with a national bank system to cope with the vastly enlarged financial needs wrought by the war. The Homestead Act of 1862, long opposed by the South, opened Western lands to cheap purchase by settlers and speculators alike.

The Pacific Railroad acts of 1862 and 1864 set in motion the construction of the first transcontinental railroad that was finally completed in 1869. The Immigration Act of 1864 encouraged the flow of newcomers and revealed the support of businessmen for liberal immigration policy to keep cheap labor flowing into the country. A host of lesser bills added their weight to fostering a climate more congenial for economic expansion than had ever existed. Four years of bitter, bloody war capped by an inconclusive peace made the

American people sick of strife and sacrifice and eager to get on with advancing their own lives.

These factors combined to make the war years a perfect breeding ground for entrepreneurs who stayed away from the killing fields. Banker Thomas Mellon impressed this point on one of his sons who was thinking of enlisting:

> I had hoped my boy was going to make a smart intelligent businessman and was not such a goose as to be *seduced from duty* by the declamations of buncombed speeches. It is only greenhorns who enlist. *You can learn nothing in the army.* ... In time you will come to understand and believe that a man may be a patriot without risking his own life or sacrificing his health. There are plenty of other lives less valuable or ready to serve for the love of serving.

While many might question this definition of patriotism, the men on our list shared this general belief. Few tried to enlist, fewer still stayed home because of disability (James J. Hill was one; he had a blind eye), and several hired substitutes. "I was represented in the army," insisted John D. Rockefeller years later. "I sent more than twenty men, yes, nearly thirty. That is, I made such arrangements for them that they were able to go."

This generation of entrepreneurs stayed home because the war itself offered fabulous opportunities that would never come again. They turned national tragedy to their advantage in four ways. Some grew rich through business coups that directly utilized wartime conditions. Others built fortunes through government contracts for supplies and services. Bankers in particular profited from the abnormal financial conditions wrought by the war and the need to finance its enormous costs. Finally, everyone gained invaluable business experience by operating in the strained, frantic arena of wartime. These lessons alone telescoped their learning years and prepared them for larger, more ambitious leaps once the war ended.

Philip Armour pulled off a lucrative speculation in pork during the war. John D. Rockefeller grew wealthy as a commission merchant in Cleveland before opening his first refinery in 1863; two years later, joined by brother William, he went entirely into the oil business. Clement Studebaker used war orders to build what became the world's largest wagon works. Andrew Carnegie served an apprenticeship on the Pennsylvania Railroad under Thomas A. Scott and learned enough to make nearly $1 million on outside investments of his own. Working out of his brother's Philadelphia meat shop, Peter Widener won a government contract to supply nearby troops and managed to accumulate $50,000 for postwar investment in other enterprises. John Wanamaker opened a clothing store in 1861 and swam happily in a flood of orders for uniforms.

In 1862 Gustavus Swift opened a retail butcher shop in Barnstable, Massachusetts, and Frederick Weyerhauser was busy organizing a logging and lumbering enterprise in Illinois and Wisconsin. Marshall Field moved from manager of one mercantile firm in 1861 to partner in another two years later. George Pullman obtained his first patent on a sleeping car in 1864. A. J. Cassatt left a railroad project in Georgia when the war started and went to the Pennsylvania Railroad, where he spent his entire career. James J. Hill learned the ropes of business and transportation working for a Mississippi River steamboat outfit. Frederick Pabst served as a steamer captain on the Great Lakes before taking up brewing in 1865.

These are but a few of many examples culled from an unusually hardy generation of entrepreneurs. All these men endured the peculiar social and moral climate of a long and exhausting war that put personal priorities into focus in a way unmatched by the routines of peacetime. Most of them emerged from the war with a fine appreciation of life's fragility and with a fierce determination to succeed. They did not need soldiering to become the most rugged of individuals or dogged in their pursuit of objectives.

Standing on the threshold of the postwar era, with the massive adjustments of demobilization and reconstruction looming on one side and the resources of the West waiting to be developed on the other, they were truly the right men in the right place at the right time. So well did they take up the challenge that their efforts changed forever the ground rules by which the game was played. The key to their success lay in mastering a characteristic that was already becoming distinctly American: organization.

To understand what they did and what happened as a result of it, consider the following scenario. It begins with an entrepreneur who has an idea that might make money. His scheme might be a new invention, an improved machine or process, a new product, or an innovation in production or distribution. He organizes a business and, to get the capital he needs, acquires one or more partners. At first the partners must do everything themselves. They must figure out how to make their product as cheaply and efficiently as possible, how to sell it, to whom, and at what price.

In solving the problems of finance, production, and marketing, their methods are loose and informal, their organization small and flexible. Everyone does several jobs, and much of what they do is improvised because they are new at it and have few precedents to go by. They operate out of a small office or even their homes and keep much of the vital information in their heads. Along the way they make mistakes and learn from them. If their product fails, they chalk it up to experience and turn to something else. But if it is a success, a host of new problems awaits them.

Their first impulse is to expand production, which requires more capital. If they want to operate on a grand scale they will probably form a corporation to raise money and hedge their personal losses should things go sour. The partners sell shares to the public, taking care to keep enough for themselves to retain control, and become managing officers in the new company. They buy new machinery and equipment, hire more people, and install the whole operation in a new building. The business can no longer be run in their heads or out of their desks on a casual basis. To cope with this expansion, the partners each take charge of certain responsibilities and hire assistants to help them.

Gradually there emerges a managerial staff arranged in a chain of command that separates the partners and their assistants from the workmen in the plant. Every staff member assumes a specialized function, and procedures such as accounting, purchasing, marketing, and production are formalized and systemized to keep track of everything as the scale of operation increases. If success continues, the business grows even larger and more complicated. New products are added, which may require separate divisions or even separate corporations to oversee them. More plants are built, and competing firms are bought out.

The amount of capital invested reaches astronomical proportions as the company becomes a national concern with salesmen opening up markets across the continent and even overseas. Divisions beget more divisions, each of which may acquire subsidiaries as well. A huge organization now towers over the original idea. By this time the partners have long passed the point where they can do or even oversee everything. They retreat to imposing offices attended by an army of clerks, typists, junior officers, and functionaries. Relieved of production details, they now devote their energies to broad questions of policy and strategy.

At this point the partners are far too busy administering their empire to promote new ideas. Every aspect of the operation has become specialized. Some officers and their staffs devote their entire time to financial matters; others tend strictly to production, marketing, technology, transportation, purchasing, research, personnel, labor relations, and public relations. The company may even hire specialists to study its administrative structure and production methods to improve efficiency. Planning and coordination have become crucial to smooth functioning, yet growth has made them more difficult to obtain.

In their twilight years and facing retirement, the partners have seen their original idea mushroom into a huge enterprise with a life of its own that transcends its founders. When the partners retire or die, their departure will be mourned and their accomplishments noted, but the company will scarcely feel their absence. Handsome portraits of them will be hung in the corporate headquarters, where they will gather dust and occasional glances from people of a generation too far removed from their achievement to appreciate what it was or what it meant.

This scenario may not fit the exact history of any particular company, but it does represent the pattern by which small companies grow into giant corporations. The process lay at the heart of the transformation of the United States from an agrarian to an industrial society. Ironically, this organizational revolution was for the most talented entrepreneurs both their supreme goal and their ultimate doom. In realizing their most far-reaching ambitions, they rendered themselves all but obsolete.

# 3

# The Corporate Economy

> Take from me all the ore mines, railroads, manufac-
> turing plants and leave me my organization, and in
> a few years I promise to duplicate the Carnegie
> Company.
>
> —Andrew Carnegie

IN JULY 1896 *Scientific American* conducted a poll to
determine which invention of the past fifty years had con-
ferred the greatest benefit on mankind. The winner, to the
surprise of some, was Bessemer steel. From the availability of
strong, cheap steel had sprung everything from locomotives
to bridges to buildings to machines of every kind, large and
small. Andrew Carnegie was the man who did more to
maximize the production of cheap steel in the United States
than any other person. As his own words indicate, the key to
his success lay in the organization he created.

As early as the 1830s Alexis de Tocqueville caught a
glimmer of the future. "In no country," he wrote, "has the
principle of association been more successfully used or
applied to a greater multitude of objects than in America."
He was referring chiefly to political organizations; between
1850 and 1920, however, an organizational revolution re-
vamped the basic structure of American civilization in ways
that affected every aspect of people's lives. In that short time

a society of individuals was transformed into a society of organizations.

This revolution proceeded along two distinct lines. First, the forms of existing organizations were radically altered and new ones devised; then the principles of organization were extended into other areas of human activity. The driving force behind these changes was a growing realization that the emerging industrial order could not function on the casual, freewheeling basis that had long characterized most of American life. The more specialized and complicated activities became, the more they required planning and coordination to operate efficiently. Improvisation, which Americans had elevated to an art form, still had its place, but not in a complex industrial system. Grudgingly, it gave way to systemization and integration.

Most Americans were startled as these changes crept over their lives because they never saw them coming. No one planned the organizational revolution; it occurred through drift rather than design and was shaped by necessity more than desire. There was no sudden, sweeping change but rather a steady process of accretion, the accumulation of countless decisions made and actions taken by people who gave little thought to the broader consequences of their actions. It originated in the economy, where ambitious entrepreneurs created industrial enterprises of awesome size and then had to find ways of administering them.

Their success at this work reshaped the structure of economic institutions in the United States. The old level playing field, with its large number of small firms, gave way to a jagged terrain dominated by huge companies in many sectors. As late as the Civil War no one could have foreseen that the corporation would become the centerpiece of American civilization. The overwhelming number of businesses still belonged to one person and usually died when he or she did. In this small-town world of individuals, business was as personal as other activities. The reputation of any firm was no more or less than that of its owner, so closely were they identified with each other.

Within this world of local companies could be found three forms of business organization. In the *proprietorship* one person owned and managed the entire operation. The *partnership* involved two or more people owning part of the business and sharing in its management. The *unincorporated shareholder company* was based upon a written agreement among shareholders, each of whom owned a part of the business and could leave it by selling his shares. The shareholders sometimes hired managers to run the operation, but the company was private and had no legal status beyond the written pact on which it was founded.

These forms were all simple, direct, and personal. They suited an economy of small firms serving local markets, but they had serious defects for larger enterprises such as a railroad. How could a small group raise the large amount of capital needed among themselves? Even if they could, the death of a partner dissolved the firm and created a legal tangle; so might a disagreement among them. Most important, all these forms had unlimited liability, which meant that every partner was personally responsible for the debts of the company. If a man's company was at the mercy of his personal reputation, so was his personal fortune at the mercy of his company.

The corporation solved all these problems. Since it had to be chartered by the state, it held a clear legal status and a separate identity from the founders. As a creature of law it outlived the owners and was not affected by their deaths. Ownership could easily be transferred through sale of shares without disturbing operations. Large amounts of capital could be raised by selling shares or issuing bonds against its property. The liability of the owners was limited to their shares in the company; the corporation's debts belonged to it and not to them.

Corporations had been around a long time, but their use had undergone several changes. Their origins lay in England, where they were conceived as a device for furthering government policy by granting special privileges in unusual cases. In America they remained this same instrument of public policy even after the Revolution; nearly all the 326 corporate charters granted by states between 1775 and 1801 were for public or quasi-public undertakings such as water works, wharves, turnpikes, banks, and insurance companies.

Then the attitude toward corporations underwent a profound shift as entrepreneurs, seeking funds for large projects like railroads, agitated to have them broadened from a limited privilege to a universal right. Critics feared that such impersonal organizations would create a divided ethic that applied one set of standards to business and another to personal matters. Peter C. Brooks of Boston warned bluntly, "Corporations will do what individuals would not dare to do," but no amount of hand-wringing could deflect the movement. Connecticut led the way by passing a general incorporation law in 1837; by 1850 most other states had followed suit.

By the time of the Civil War the corporation had been transformed from a specially granted instrument of public policy into a general vehicle for private enterprise. Nearly half of all corporate charters issued before 1860 were granted during the 1850s. While most firms continued to incorporate under special legislative acts rather than general statutes because they could often obtain special privileges that way, the idea prevailed that incorporation was little more than a formal licensing function. After the war corporations emerged as the structural norm for large enterprises because they could operate efficiently on a scale that would overwhelm even the most intelligent partnership.

During the first two decades after the Civil War, the major large corporations continued to be railroads, which were expanding at a dizzying rate, keeping busy the industries that supplied them and lowering the cost of shipping for hundreds of other industries. Once-small banking firms on Wall Street grew rich handling the huge outpouring of securities issued by railroads to finance their growth, giving rise to a large and powerful investment banking industry. As late as the 1880s the listings on the New York Stock Exchange consisted overwhelmingly of railroad securities along with some utilities and a few manufacturing stocks. But that pattern was in the process of changing as more industrial and manufacturing firms switched from partnerships or proprietorships to corporations.

The reasons for their switch lay in two closely related factors: growth and competition. In the older world of many small companies serving local markets, competition among firms was seldom a decisive factor. But new technologies, sources of fuel, and improved production techniques enabled companies to increase output, and an expanding rail system provided access to distant markets. As more capital was invested to expand production, the need to capture regional and later national markets became imperative. And as firms moved beyond their local markets to a broader arena, they had to compete not only with local producers in the new region but also with other firms doing the same thing. The result was a new and more lethal kind of competition.

Bright and ambitious entrepreneurs reveled in the possibilities offered by expansion. They might capture distant markets by displacing local firms and shutting out other distant rivals, perhaps even dominate a major portion of the industry. This required a large, efficient central organization capable of producing huge quantities at the lowest possible costs and selling in far-flung markets at the lowest possible prices. The key to success lay in a corporation that could manage all these functions because it alone could command the resources necessary to conduct operations on so unprecedented a scale.

Here too railroads pioneered the pattern as they expanded from short local lines into integrated through lines and then into complex systems. Most local lines were financed and built by local interests to serve their own communities. As these roads were bought and absorbed by larger companies, ownership passed into hands that often had little presence and less interest in the local communities other than as a source of business. One result of this change was a growing local hostility toward the railroad by local shippers who thought it charged too high rates.

This same pattern had even more far-reaching effects when it was repeated by industrial and manufacturing firms. Local butchers in a town competed for sales but seldom drove each other out of business in the process. But once Gustavus Swift, Philip D. Armour, and others built giant meat-packing enterprises, they competed with local butchers as well as each other in hundreds of towns across the nation. If one of the giants came off badly in a local market, he had plenty of other places in which to rebound. Not so the local butchers, who were often squeezed out of business by the giant firms.

Even the giants started small and grew large by winning the competitive wars at local and regional levels. John D. Rockefeller entered the oil refining business in 1863 partly because it offered large profits for a relatively small investment. But so did many other people. "Naturally all sorts of people went into it," he observed later; "the butcher, the baker, the candlestick maker began to refine oil, and it was only a matter of time before more of the finished product was put on the market than could possibly be consumed."

At that point the industry entered a stage of desperate competition as each company struggled to capture the largest possible share of the market. This could only be done at the expense of competing firms and required some decisive advantage, such as lower costs through more efficient production methods or some new technology or goods of superior quality. The path to a competitive edge was clear: buy raw materials cheaper, pay lower wages, get lower transportation rates, gain superior marketing arrangements. Sometimes these goals could be achieved openly and legally, but often secret and illegal or unethical methods were employed.

Since every company sought the same advantages, the result was usually a vicious competitive brawl marked by price wars, fights over patents, protracted legal suits, even industrial sabotage. The struggle plunged whole industries into disorder. Railroad rate wars and practices such as rebating (giving special rates secretly to preferred shippers) disturbed both transportation costs and marketing arrangements. Legal battles over charters and other forms of privileged legislation led companies into the nether world of political bribery and corruption to get what they wanted and keep rivals from getting what they desired.

Observers labeled this type of warfare "cutthroat competition" and branded it the most rugged form of individualism. While businessmen paid homage to these values in public, privately they found them intolerable. Cutthroat competition bred waste, inefficiency, and, worst of all, instability. It threw industries into chaos and prevented businessmen from conducting their enterprise on a rational basis by unsettling all their calculations on costs, production, and marketing. The lesson was clear: to survive and grow, businessmen had to minimize competition.

The obvious way to reduce competition was to eliminate competitors by buying them out or driving them out of business. Growth was thus the result of two closely linked forces. It was a by-product of the competitive struggle as strong firms absorbed weaker rivals, and it was also the result of superior efficiency, resources, and organization that made some firms strong enough to seize markets from less capable opponents. In many industries—oil refining, iron and steel manufacturing, and meat packing are good examples—the strongest firms made a good product at the lowest possible cost, sold it as cheaply as possible, and ran a tight, efficient organization to maximize control.

In this manner order gradually replaced chaos. As a handful of giant firms emerged to dominate an industry, the smaller survivors found they could not compete with the giants unless they combined their resources in a larger company. The new imperative of the industrial economy announced itself with brutal clarity: organize or perish. The great entrepreneurs understood this principle well; it was no accident that Carnegie, Rockefeller, Swift, Henry O. Havemeyer, and others were all superb organizers.

This race toward organization snuffed out hordes of small local firms as corporate giants captured their markets. The general store, which had long served the vast isolated expanses of rural America, could not compete with the prices and diversity of Sears, Roebuck or Montgomery Ward. Small shops were squeezed out by department stores and chain stores in drugs, food, clothes, shoes, confectioneries, and many other areas. Everywhere local economies fell under the sway of distant corporate owners, and their products grew more standardized.

The domination of industries by giant firms also closed them to new competitors. The capital required to enter the iron and steel, oil, meat-packing, foundry, or other major industries in 1890 was enormous compared with what it had been in 1860. A group of smaller firms might combine into a new giant corporation, or some unexpected event like the fabulous Spindletop oil strikes in 1901 in Texas might thrust new competitors into the picture. But these were exceptions to a tough rule: the scale of operation and increased use of machinery rendered start-up costs too high for newcomers in already developed industries. The new entrepreneurs found their niche in other industries where the playing field was still level or as yet undefined.

The emergence of large corporations opened a new phase of the organizational revolution. In the preindustrial economy, with its large number of small firms, the outcome of a competitive struggle affected few people beyond those in the fight. When the economy began organizing around large corporate enterprises, however, the combatants were national firms serving markets spread across the entire country. Competition between them turned what had been a limited war into total war as the combat zone widened to embrace noncombatants who had earlier escaped the battle.

If this clash of arms brought down a corporate giant, its failure could throw thousands of people out of work and adversely affect subsidiary firms, suppliers, jobbers, retailers, transportation companies. Security prices might drop and the money market tighten, sending waves of contraction to batter banks and brokerages and thereby crash down on distant businesses and industries. One fearful collapse might trigger a panic or recession, or signal the onset of a major depression paralyzing the whole economy.

The period 1850–1920 witnessed two major depressions (1873–1879 and 1893–1897), two recessions (1913–1916 and 1920–1921), and severe panics in 1857, 1884, and 1907 along with several lesser panics, slumps, and financial crises. Gradually it became clear that the enlarged scale of operations in a corporate economy multiplied the impact of both success and failure upon the entire system. The diverse elements of the industrial economy became so intertwined that any major disturbance invited disaster. At this level the fallout from unrestrained competition menaced not only business but society as well.

Gradually the role of competition came full circle. As industrialization expanded it bred intense competitive struggles from which the victors grew ever larger while the losers perished or were absorbed. But an industrial system dominated by giant firms demanded stability, which meant an end to the cutthroat competition that had produced it. Size enabled firms to produce more goods with greater efficiency at lower cost if they did not dissipate their strength on warfare. Large companies could raise capital more easily or generate it from earnings; they could afford to invest more money in research, technicians, patents, and new products. Giant corporations could also exert more political leverage.

But size brought weaknesses as well. The larger an enterprise grew, the more difficult became coordination and communication within it. Large organizations required elaborate administrative structures that kept track of operations in a formal, organized manner. This in turn gave rise to what Alfred D. Chandler, Jr., called "a new subspecies of economic man," the salaried manager. These managers found it harder to maintain efficiency and instill a clear sense of direction in employees who had lost all contact with the owners of the firm and whose jobs had grown steadily more specialized and detached from a finished product. The age of bureaucracy, with all its headaches, had dawned.

Large operations also required a huge capital investment, most of it in fixed costs like plant and equipment. These costs must be paid regardless of whether the company sold any goods. If business slowed, management could slow production and lay off workers, but it could not ignore rent, utilities, interest payments, or taxes. These fixed costs, unlike variable costs (wages, raw materials), continued despite changes in output or sales. To maximize profits, therefore, large firms had to produce steadily and as near to full capacity as possible, since many of their costs continued when production fell off.

Once regularity of output became as important as efficiency of output, companies found themselves under pressure to sell goods whether or not there existed enough buyers for their product. If the demand was not there, it must be generated; if the market was inadequate, it must be developed. By the 1870s several key industries had grown so large and efficient that their productive capacity began to exceed demand. This led to recurring cycles of recession and depression, price declines and fluctuations, and chronic overproduction in some sectors of the economy.

Many companies responded by slashing prices to get whatever business they could, believing it was better to get some business at a small profit (or even loss) than to sell nothing. From this premise flowed the worst of cutthroat competition. Railroads especially battered one another into bankruptcy, but price-slashing infected oil, iron and steel, and dozens of other industries. Small firms lacked the resources to sustain a long fight, but even large companies recoiled at the waste and uncertainty of prolonged price battles.

Some way had to be found to eliminate competition and the instability it bred. Two different approaches were tried: collusion and combination. Collusive agreements took several forms, most of them secret pacts among two or more major competitors. The best known of these devices, the industrial pool, sought to maintain prices and sometimes included provisions to divide markets on a prorated basis, control output, restrict patents, and combine services or sales agencies. The railroads made the most extensive use of pools, but the rope, wallpaper, whiskey, and other industries also resorted to them.

Pools seldom worked satisfactorily because they had fatal flaws. They lacked any standing in common or statutory law and so could not be enforced. They amounted to gentlemen's agreements among men not known for their gentlemanly behavior. Few pool members hesitated to violate the agreement if it served their interests, especially in hard times. "A starving man will usually get bread if it is to be had," declared rail magnate James J. Hill, "and a starving railway will not maintain rates." The pool also ran afoul of laws governing restraint of trade, and the Interstate Commerce Act of 1887 explicitly prohibited them for railroads.

By that time most business leaders had discarded collusion in favor of combination as the surest road to stability. Combination could proceed in two very different directions. In *horizontal integration* a company sought to acquire or merge with other direct competitors. Standard Oil, which refined petroleum, bought up other refineries until it dominated the refining process. The other approach, *vertical integration*, saw a company reach backward to control its suppliers and/or forward to dominate finishing processes, distribution, and marketing. In this case Standard Oil moved to acquire oil fields, pipelines, barrel manufacturers, warehouses, transportation and docking facilities, retail outlets, and other businesses crucial to the production and sale of petroleum.

Vertical integration stabilized the entire production process. It assured a steady flow of raw materials at predictable prices, guaranteed regular transportation connections, and provided a reliable network for distributing and selling the finished product. The company could function like a well-oiled machine with minimal risk of interruption or breakdown. Vertical integration could also produce real economies, greater efficiency, better quality control, and more dependable production schedules.

Where vertical integration stabilized the production process, horizontal integration stabilized the industry itself by eliminating competitors. The object was not to create a monopoly, which never really existed in any major industry, but rather an oligopoly in which two or more giant firms dominated in a way that assured stable prices without cutthroat competition. Horizontal integration had little effect on production efficiency or excess capacity, and it attracted more public attention. Most of the public outcry that arose against "trusts" and "monopolies" was directed at companies that employed this approach.

The quest for stability drove American entrepreneurs relentlessly down the path of combination and merger. Their efforts to extend control over entire industries led them to devise two new forms of organization, the trust and the holding company. These legal innovations transformed the structure of American business and revealed the changing conditions of business enterprise. Both attacked a basic obstacle: the common-law prohibition against one corporation holding stock in another without a specific sanction in law to do so. This obstacle prevented one firm from legally controlling another or coordinating their functions.

The trust tried to skirt this obstacle by exchanging the stock of every subsidiary company for certificates of trust, which were held by a group of trustees. If the same group of trustees served all the subsidiary companies, they had practical control over them. Standard Oil pioneered this approach in the early 1880s, and its formidable success made "trust" a public scare-word for giantism in business. Critics saw trusts looming around every corner, but a later search by Alfred D. Chandler, Jr., found only eight that had actually operated in the national market. Two of these, in cattle and cordage, soon folded; the other six—petroleum, linseed oil, cottonseed oil, sugar, whiskey, and lead processing—remained atop their industries for decades.

The trust device was cumbersome and quickly ran afoul of state and federal courts as well as state legislatures. The holding company was a far simpler device in which a parent company, which produced no goods but existed only to hold securities in other companies, exchanged its shares for those of subsidiary companies. Through this device control over any number of companies could be exerted by owning the parent company. The problem was that a charter for any holding company could be secured only by a special act of the state legislature.

The obvious solution was for states to create general incorporation laws sanctioning holding companies just as they had done earlier with corporations. New Jersey led the way by passing such an act in 1889; other states soon followed, but New Jersey established itself as the home base of several large corporations (including Standard Oil) seeking to unify far-flung interests into one cohesive empire. The new law allowed corporations to capitalize at any amount and to own property and operate in other states as well as own stock in other corporations.

This liberality marked an important milestone in the organizational revolution as companies rushed to utilize the new structure. Between 1890 and 1910 a trickle of mergers swelled into a flood, fixing in one generation the basic structure of the American economy for the next century. The previous twenty years of competitive struggle had produced impressive growth by many firms but only twelve real giants with a combined capitalization of less than $1 billion. Between 1895 and 1904, according to economist Ralph L. Nelson, there were 319 mergers with a total capitalization of more than $6 billion. A mere 29 mergers accounted for 40 percent of that amount; one company alone, United States Steel, was capitalized at $1.37 billion, or 23 percent of the total.

United States Steel became the largest corporation in the nation. The age of colossal companies had dawned, and the merger mania helped feed their rise. During this same decade an average of 301 companies vanished each year into a merger; in 1899 alone, 1,028 firms disappeared. Combination was no guarantee of success; a study of 328 mergers between 1888 and 1906 found that 62 of them later failed. Other firms, however, marched toward giantism by following up horizontal integration with administrative centralization and then vertical integration.

By 1900 the pattern had become clear: the age of enterprise had given birth to the age of organizations. The saplings of individual initiative had grown into a mighty forest of corporate bureaucracies whose towering presence left little sunlight to nourish ambitious young sprouts. The demonic energy of a generation of entrepreneurs had wrought an organizational revolution that was fast dooming their breed to extinction. No one grasped this more clearly than John D. Rockefeller, who gave the era its epitaph:

> This movement was the origin of the whole modern economic administration. It has revolutionized the way of doing business all over the world. The time was ripe for it. It had to come, though all we saw at the moment was the need to save ourselves from wasteful competition.... The day of combination is here to stay. Individualism is gone, never to return.

# 4

# The Business of Farming

> Burn down your cities and leave our farms, and
> your cities will spring up again as if by magic; but
> destroy our farms and the grass will grow in the
> streets of every city in the country.
> —William Jennings Bryan (1896)

FROM THE BEGINNING, American life was firmly
rooted in the soil. In a preindustrial world, where land was
the principal source of wealth and power, the vast American
continent offered settlers a unique opportunity to carve out
their own destinies in a way not possible in Europe. After
the American Revolution new policies were devised to dis-
tribute land more widely and rapidly to eager settlers.
Farming became the backbone of American society as well
as of its economy. Whether toiling a patch of rocky ground
in New England or managing a South Carolina plantation,
those who worked the soil fashioned not only a living but a
way of life as well.

The farmer emerged early as the symbol of the young
republic. Americans like Thomas Jefferson and foreign
observers alike rhapsodized over the image of the sturdy
yeoman behind the plow, earning his own livelihood on his
own land. No one did more to implant the agrarian myth
than Jefferson, who once went so far as to predict that the
sheer size of the American continent would make it unnec-

essary for manufacturing even to exist here because every man could have his own plot of land. "Those who labor in the earth," he wrote, "are the chosen people of God, if ever he had a chosen people, whose breasts He has made His peculiar deposit for substantial and genuine virtue."

The farmer was all the things Americans imagined themselves to be: independent, self-reliant, imbued with a common sense born of experience that served him well in public affairs. But this image contained both a fateful paradox and a fatal contradiction. The contradiction was slavery, which originally surfaced in many colonies but gradually took root in the Southern states, where slave labor was deemed crucial to producing crops on a large scale. Nothing played more havoc with American values than the presence of slavery in a society that called itself free and democratic.

The paradox went to the root of the farmer's most cherished image of himself. He was the emblem of independence and self-reliance in a society that revered these traits, yet he worked at an occupation that left him utterly dependent upon factors beyond his control. The farmer could not know for certain how much of what he planted would come to harvest. He was helpless before the whims of nature ranging from rainfall to frosts, storms, floods, and insect plagues. He could not control or even influence the price he got for his crop or his access to market or his costs for such things as transportation and storage. Everything he did was ordained by the rhythm of the seasons, from which he could not deviate, and the outcome of his labors was always a roll of the dice.

These factors made farming one of the toughest and riskiest of businesses. The hours were long, the work hard, and the pay uncertain. Living conditions were often crude and always isolated, yet Americans took up farming eagerly because it promised not only a living but a way of life that allowed a family to make its way on its own land. To many eyes the farmer seemed entirely self-sufficient in his ability to grow or raise most of the things he needed. But every farmer needed some cash for necessary items and could only obtain it by selling some part of his output. Once a farmer sold his product in the marketplace, be it a small amount of potatoes or milk or the harvest of a huge rice plantation, he became a commercial farmer to that extent. Over time most farmers moved toward exchanging their crops for cash and thereby entered the market economy.

Industrialization revolutionized farming no less than it did other aspects of American life, but often in ways more indirect than direct. The transformation began before the Civil War with the gradual appearance of machinery and the thrust of railroads westward that opened new lands to settlement. The coming of the railroad and the telegraph transformed the marketing and financing of the country's most important products, grain and cotton, during the 1850s, and extended their influence to other commodities after the Civil War. Besides moving crops to market much faster, the rail and telegraph system also made possible the rise of satellite enterprises such as grain elevators, warehouses, cotton presses, and commodity exchanges.

Two Midwestern states illustrate how these forces operated. During the 1850s the populations of Illinois and Wisconsin doubled, and their output of crops grew even more spectacularly. In Illinois the wheat crop jumped from 9.4 million bushels in 1849 to 23.8 million in 1859, while corn output leaped from 57.6 million bushels to 115 million. Wheat produced in Wisconsin soared from 4.2 million bushels to 15.6 million. Still more wheat poured in from the farther reaches of Minnesota and Iowa.

Much of this output flowed into Chicago, which emerged as the leading grain terminal in the nation, and Milwaukee.

In 1850 the still raw frontier town of Chicago handled 834,000 bushels of wheat and 469,000 bushels of corn. A decade later the figures had mushroomed to 12.4 million bushels of wheat and 13.7 million of corn. In that same time Milwaukee's receipts of wheat jumped from 298,000 bushels to nearly 7.6 million. From these cities the grain traveled across the Great Lakes to Buffalo for consignment eastward via the Erie Canal or rail. Although the grain left Chicago by boat, 75 percent of it arrived there from the West by train.

By 1860 a new transportation and distribution system was already in place in the Northwest. A steadily expanding rail network fed growing shipments of grain, meat, and other products into Chicago, where they were loaded onto boats and sent eastward over the lakes. Huge storage elevators were built to handle the mountain of grain; the first elevator in Chicago went up in 1848 and was quickly followed by others. Buffalo, too, lined its lakefront with elevators to receive the grain, enabling it to handle far greater quantities than was possible under the old system of putting it in sacks.

The new system reduced storage and transportation costs as well as eliminating the farmer's dependence on local monopolies of millers and merchants. The greatest benefits went to the most distant growers, for whom transportation and storage comprised a larger part of their total costs. As a result, the center of wheat production shifted steadily westward to the vast stretches of prairie opening up, forcing smaller producers in more urbanized regions to switch to other crops. A similar pattern of westward movement occurred with cotton production in the South, but for an entirely different reason. The once fertile lands of the seaboard had been exhausted by overfarming, depleting not only the soil but the local economy as well.

Then came the Civil War, which radically transformed American farming in ways no one could have foreseen. It changed not only the rules of the game but the playing field as well. Most obviously, it destroyed the Southern plantation system with its dependence on slave labor. The war devastated many regions of the South, leaving farms without animals or implements, with run-down barns and buildings, and with the massive social problem of freed slaves whose place in society had not yet been defined. From this debris emerged a primitive system based on farm tenancy and sharecropping, which had the effect of binding black and white farmers alike to the land for the benefit of its owner.

The effect of the war on the North was much different but no less profound. The war's demand for food and manpower hastened the spread of machinery to replace human labor. As men marched off to war, women, children, and older men took their places in the field. Farm machinery manufacturers sniffed bonanza profits in the wind. The most astute of them, Cyrus McCormick, reminded a salesman in Illinois, "Don't be so blue over prospects. Remember 20,000 militia have to leave this state...and these men will have to come, many or a large share of them, from the farms."

By 1860 early versions of harrows, planters, mowers, reapers, and threshers, along with new types of plows, had appeared, but mowers and reapers were still relatively new. In 1864, however, mower production reached seventy thousand, or twice the output of 1862, while McCormick alone turned out six thousand reapers in 1864. "This year the demand for reapers has been so great," noted *Scientific American* in 1863, "that manufacturers will not be able to fill their orders. Farming is comparatively child's play to what it was twenty years ago."

The results were impressive. Northern farms produced enough corn, wheat, and oats to fill domestic needs and still sell huge quantities to England for badly needed exchange. Hog and cattle output also rose sharply, and the number of sheep doubled during the war, sending wool production from 60 million pounds in 1860 to 140 million in 1865. The bumper crop of wool went a long way in replacing the cotton supply lost when the South seceded. Northern agriculture emerged from the war in booming condition and cheerfully addicted to the use of machinery to boost production.

The war also enabled a Republican Congress to pass two key pieces of land legislation in 1862, the Homestead Act and the Morrill Act, which granted every loyal state thirty thousand acres of land to endow an agricultural college. When the war ended, an army of settlers (including many former soldiers) streamed westward to start life anew on government land. Congress also gave huge parcels of land to railroads, much of which was used to lure settlers along the rail line. In 1864, for example, the Atchison, Topeka & Santa Fe Railroad sold sixty thousand acres to German-Russian Mennonites who migrated to Kansas.

The dimensions of this westward movement can be seen in one fact: American farmers put more land under cultivation between 1867 and 1900 than they had in the whole previous history of the country since 1607. Production shifted steadily westward. In 1869 the farmland west of the 95th meridian (roughly Kansas City) produced only 6 percent of the nation's total crops; by 1909 that figure had risen to 30 percent.

The opening of so much new acreage had far-reaching consequences. It accelerated the process of specialization by forcing more Eastern farmers to abandon the staple crops grown in the West and find other niches in the food market. "The New England farmer has found his products selling at lower prices because of the new, fierce and rapidly increasing competition," noted one authority in 1890. "One by one he has had to abandon the growing of this or that crop because the West crowded him beyond the paying point." Eastern farmers turned to truck farming and dairying; New York state led the nation in dairy products until Wisconsin surpassed it during the 1910s. Wisconsin began to specialize in dairying after its farmers could no longer grow wheat profitably in competition with Western farms.

This competition, coupled with the hunger for land and need for new machinery, turned most practitioners of necessity into commercial farmers. As historian John T. Schlebecker observed, "Technology and science seemed to dominate American agriculture from 1861 to 1914. Farmers had to sell their produce at prices high enough to afford the new technology. Therefore, effective marketing was necessary for the adoption of new methods, equipment, chemicals, plants, and animals." The sturdy yeoman behind the plow found himself increasingly forced to become a businessman, a role for which he often had little talent.

Technology had plenty to offer farmers. New types of cast iron and steel plows made that arduous task easier. The sulky plow, which spread rapidly during the 1870s, allowed the farmer to ride instead of walk behind his team and doubled the amount of ground he could cover. Disk harrows cut and turned under stubble as well as breaking up heavy soils, while seed drills put down seed economically. The checkrower and lister solved planting problems faced by corn growers. Early reapers gave way to more sophisticated models and were joined by binding machines, harvesters, threshers, mowers, and finally the combine, which did both reaping and threshing. Barbed wire provided cheap fencing for regions lacking wood or stone.

Dairy farmers too benefited from new inventions. As the historian Fred A. Shannon observed, the centrifugal cream separator and the centrifugal cream tester "did more than all others in revolutionizing the dairy industry in the later decades of the century." The new method not only saved considerable labor but also captured nearly all the cream and produced it at any thickness desired. By 1900 American farmers had more than 40,000 centrifugal separators in use. Churns too underwent steady improvement—more than 2,700 patents were issued for versions of them alone.

Sometimes advances came faster than farmers could absorb them. Harvesters spread rapidly until there were about 100,000 of them by 1879, then dwindled away within a decade as self-binding harvesters came onto the market. By one estimate the self-binder saved the labor of two men over the harvester and five men over the reaper. Threshing machines, driven by steam engines, saved the labor of two men by knocking grain free of the straw, carrying it away, elevating it, and dumping it into a haystack. Between 1880 and 1914 the capacity of threshers doubled and their functions expanded with the addition of automatic twine cutters, feeders, weighers, and blowers. Cumbersome steam engines gave way to more powerful and efficient gasoline-powered engines.

New techniques also did much to improve farming during these years. Some were learned from hard experience; others came from the new land-grant colleges funded by the Morrill Act. The region west of the 98th meridian (roughly Wichita) posed a special problem for farmers because it received much less rainfall. One solution evolved in the form of dry farming, which involved creating larger farms where half the land lay fallow each year to accumulate moisture. Prodded by the railroads, the government in 1906 added a Bureau of Dry Land Agriculture to the Department of Agriculture. Farmers also learned to improve the soil through use of fertilizers and rotation of crops. The introduction of silos in 1873 allowed grass and other plant stalks to be stored and converted by biochemical reaction into excellent feed for animals. Important advances were made in the prevention of diseases like pleuropneumonia in cattle and hog cholera.

The mushrooming westward movement tied distant farmers ever more to their lifeline of rails and to the new marketing system that had evolved to make mass agricultural production possible. Where the railroad provided access to markets, the telegraph accelerated the flow of information about crops and their movements. It enabled the new commodities exchanges to systematize marketing procedures, improve methods of financing, and reduce the costs of moving crops by allowing them to be bought and sold before they were shipped or even harvested.

The new system came first to the grain trade. Historian John G. Clark explained it this way:

> The telegraph put western markets in close touch with price changes in eastern centers, and the railroads facilitated delivery so that a favorable price change could be exploited. As a result, larger purchases of grain were made in markets such as Chicago and Buffalo. With the aid of telegraphic communication, a dealer in New York could also purchase directly at the point of production. The degree of risk, though still large, was lessened.... More important, as the time required for a shipment of grain to arrive at its destination was reduced, so too was the time in which the purchaser was overextended by an advance.

New storage and shipment methods required standardized grading of wheat as well as facilities for weighing and inspection. The Chicago Board of Trade, founded in 1848, assumed these tasks during the 1850s, as did similar bodies in other cities. From their efforts arose a set of national standards for these functions. A new form of contract, the "to arrive" or futures agreement, gave rise to practices that helped stabilize prices, lower credit costs, and shift much of the risk in shipments to speculators on grain exchanges. Commodity dealers replaced the merchants who had once dominated the grain trade. A similar pattern reshaped the marketing of cotton, and later corn, rye, oats, and barley as well.

Given the times, the new technologies, and the availability of cheap land, it is hardly surprising that some ambitious men conceived notions about farming as grand as those in the corporate world. During the 1880s these dreamers founded what became known as "bonanza farms" to produce crops on a mass scale. One such farm in the Red River Valley of North Dakota had a single field of wheat embracing 13,000 acres. "You are in a sea of wheat," marveled a reporter. "The railroad train rolls through an ocean of grain." Another Red River bonanza was estimated to be 61,500 acres, or five times the area of Manhattan Island. John T. Alexander, who already owned 80,000 acres of land in Illinois, bought a 23,000-acre holding and later added another 26,500 acres.

Michael L. Sullivant, who once owned 80,000 acres of land in Illinois, developed another 40,000 acres on which he planted 18,000 acres in corn and 5,000 acres in other crops. Within five years his corn yield reached 450,000 bushels. His crews were armed with the newest implements, among them 150 steel plows, 75 breaking plows, 142 cultivators, 45 corn planters, 25 gang harrows, and several steam-driven corn shellers. Most bonanza farms were divided into units run by superintendents who managed gangs of migrant workers. After a brief heyday the giant farms declined during the late 1880s as rainfall and yields dwindled, prices fell, and taxes rose. Unlike smaller farms, the bonanzas could not easily shift to more diversified crops or cultivate their land more intensively.

The dream of bigness was not confined to Americans. A congressional committee found in 1886 that twenty-nine companies controlled by foreigners owned a total of 20.7 million farm acres. One English company held 3 million acres in Texas; the Holland Company owned 4.5 million acres in New Mexico. These giant holdings aroused cries of monopoly usually directed at industrial corporations and prompted the historian Paul W. Gates to label the bonanza farms "an amazing commentary upon...[a] so-called democratic land system."

Agriculture did eventually turn into big business, but not along the lines feared by late-nineteenth-century critics. It was not possible for farmers to emulate the mass production techniques of manufacturing. Chandler explained why they could not:

> In the raising of...crops, biological constraints determined the time of preparing the soil, sowing, cultivating, and harvesting, and so set the speed of the overall process of production. Improved strains of crops and better fertilizers increased output per acre worked; improved machinery made it possible to carry out the different processes of production at a somewhat greater speed. But the need almost never arose to devise organizational procedures to integrate and coordinate the processes. Therefore, the family was able to remain the basic agricultural working unit; and the farmer, his family, and a handful of hired helpers relied, until the twentieth century, on human and animal power to work farm implements and machines.

The contrast between industry and agriculture can be seen clearly in the new process flour mills that arose during the 1870s. Two of these mills could grind in one day the wheat grown on 225,000 acres of land. It was to keep these mills supplied on a reliable basis with eight to ten carloads of wheat daily that the new transportation and commodities marketing systems arose. No amount of technology or technique could enable wheat growers to match such quantum leaps in processing.

The majority of farmers were small businessmen, and many suffered the fate common to small businessmen. When prices were good and rainfall plentiful, they grew buoyant and borrowed money to increase output by buying more land and equipment. But prices kept moving downward, and in the mid-1880s the weather moved into a dry cycle. Many farmers were hard pressed to stay solvent; some lost their land and worked it as tenants. In 1880 nearly 26 percent of all American farmers were sharecroppers or tenants; by 1910 the figure had jumped to 37 percent.

For all the rhetoric that extolled the virtues of farming and farm life, the farmer was in reality a businessman playing a losing game. He had no control over his output, his costs, or the price he received for his crop. He was a debtor in the nation's longest unbroken period of deflation, which favors creditors. Because the banks, country stores, railroads, elevators, machinery salesmen, and others charged him more than he could afford to pay, he assumed they were gouging him. While this may sometimes have been true, the suspicion was seldom based on actual knowledge of costs or rates or prices. The harsh truth was that these other interests could exert more control over some (but by no means all) aspects of their business than the farmer could over his.

Many farmers, like other small businessmen, failed to survive and quit the land or worked it as tenants. Unlike other small businessmen, however, farmers had a social role with roots deep in the nation's origins and values. Sturdy yeomen were the pillars of democracy, the emblems of a free society. Anything that threatened their survival went beyond personal failure to become a menace to democracy and independence themselves. To jaded urban eyes the farmer might seem more of a rube or a hick than a national icon, but the rural myth exerted a powerful hold on national values and therefore possessed political clout.

The distress of farmers was real enough, but too often their diagnosis of its causes and their proposed solutions ranged from the simplistic to the conspiratorial. From their rural perspective, the forces that assailed them seemed to erode the very structure of American life and values. Like most people, they found causes for their woes everywhere but in their own shortcomings. In particular they singled out the railroads, the elevators, the currency system, the banks, Wall Street, the new commodities exchanges, cities, and later Jews and immigrants, whose presence in their view poisoned the wellspring of American values.

It was difficult for farmers to organize, being so widely scattered and independent by nature, but organize they did. Through a series of associations and political movements they sought relief from their economic distress and betterment of their position in life. The Granger movement began in 1867 and lasted into the late 1870s, enrolling more than 858,000 members at its peak. While trying to address the farmers' economic plight, it also offered social and cultural uplift programs along with elaborate secret rituals to impart some excitement to their lives.

In some states the movement succeeded in bringing about the first regulation of railroads, with results that utterly politicized the railroad question without giving much relief to farmers. The Granges also sought to lower the cost of consumer goods for their members by eliminating middlemen. Montgomery Ward, the first catalog operation in America, was founded in 1872 specifically to do business with Grangers. In the Midwest Grangers promoted activities that had been launched even earlier, such as the founding of cooperative grain elevators and dairy cooperatives. The latter spread rapidly in New England, especially in Massachusetts.

But in the end the Grange movement could not alleviate the farmer's woes. Historians Thomas C. Cochran and William Miller offer this explanation for its failure:

> The history of the Granges is the history of the failure of makeshift organizations among independent agricultural enterprisers, in their fight against other business forces, richer, more closely integrated, more accustomed to cooperating until their objectives were achieved.

When the Grange movement languished, farmer clubs throughout many states remained active and gradually coalesced into two loose groups, the Northern Alliance and the Southern Alliance. Black farmers in the South formed their own alliance in 1886 with a membership that exceeded 1.2 million. Although differing in many respects from one another, the alliances shared the common fuel of indignant members who resented their helplessness in the face of the forces that were shaping their lives. Hard times during the late 1880s drove farmers into the alliances as they had the Granges a decade earlier. Like the Granges, the alliances promoted programs of economic, social, and educational uplift. Some attempted cooperative ventures for buying goods, marketing crops, and even manufacturing farm machinery.

The Grange and alliance movements also shared a similar destiny. Both achieved a pattern of scattered successes followed by eventual failure for two basic reasons: lack of cooperative staying power and the pitfalls of politics. As one sympathizer admitted, "Some of the farmers cannot or will not pull together." An alliance lecturer, speaking on the failure of farmers to support their own cooperative ventures, touched the heart of the matter:

> The question of failure or success depends upon whether honesty and business methods are combined in the man-

agement. Failures have more generally resulted from lack of applying business methods in the conduct of business. Too often have farmers... rushed into the formation of a joint company for the purpose of conducting a co-operative store. The company... [is] placed under the direction of a man who has no business experience nor aptitude for business. The result is business failure, and general disorganization of the farmers.

Most farmers, like most small businessmen, were simply not good enough at business to succeed at what was undeniably a very tough business. Nor were they any better at politics, at least in the beginning. Given their own views on the sources of their distress, farmers could not expect to improve their lot without using their combined strength in the political arena. It might have grated on the self-image of the proud, independent farmer to ask government for help or even join a movement seeking action, but hard times left him little choice. The real dilemma of all the farm movements was not *whether* to exert their political muscle but *how* best to use it. On this question Grangers and alliancemen alike fell into the same classic snare of American politics.

This was the dilemma of whether to seek political action within the existing parties or form a new party centered on farm needs. Unlike their European counterparts, American political parties were not founded on specific ideologies or issues. The membership of both the Democratic and Republican parties embraced a broad spectrum of beliefs, from radical to conservative, as well as a rainbow of specific interests. Only in this way could a party hope to attract a broad enough constituency to win a national election. What the party stood for—besides winning elections and providing its members the spoils of victory—depended on which elements controlled the party at any given time.

From this tendency evolved a distinctive pattern of American politics in which national parties survived by avoiding strong stands on tough issues that might divide their ranks. Whenever a controversial issue rose to prominence, the two national parties tended to draw closer together in common refusal to take a decisive stand on it. This refusal led advocates of the issue to form a third party dedicated to achieving their goals. Third parties had the advantage of a clear purpose—everyone knew where they stood—and the fatal flaw of a narrow constituency. This posed a further dilemma: to remain constant a third party had to keep its ideals pure; to broaden its appeal and support base, however, it had to dilute its original stand and embrace other issues as well.

The national parties faced a similar problem. If the issue underlying the third party was potent enough, it might siphon large numbers of supporters from a major party. To undercut this threat, one of the national parties usually shifted its position to embrace a mild version of the issue staked out by the third party. In this way the issue entered the political mainstream in watered-down form and the third party faded away, having lost the battle but won the war. But the process did not always work this smoothly. If the issue was so disruptive and the positions on it so implacable that milder versions proved unacceptable, it might shatter one or both of the national parties.

Slavery had precisely this effect as every attempt to force the issue out of national politics failed miserably. It destroyed the Whig party, from the ruins of which the new Republican party emerged, and splintered the Democrats into what became the minority party until well into the next century. When no compromise could be found on the incendiary issue of slavery, civil war followed. No other major issue has wrought such devastation on American life or divided Americans so neatly along geographical lines.

The agrarian protest movements followed this same basic pattern and stumbled over its intractable dilemmas. Both the Granges and the alliances stopped short of direct political action at first, preferring to let their members work for change within the existing political parties. Both major parties paid lip service to the farmer's needs, but neither yielded power to its agrarian wing. In desperation farmers twice sought relief from third parties: the short-lived Greenback party (1874–1884) and the Populist party, formed in 1890 and made official two years later.

Both the Greenbackers and the Populists aspired to be broad-based reform parties only to find themselves fighting for victory over the narrow issue of currency reform. The Populists put together an improbable coalition of interests but could not build a stable political base on the mix. In 1896 the party chose to use the currency or silver issue to cement widespread support in the presidential campaign. To the party's chagrin, the Democrats coopted its position, leaving the Populists a no-win choice of supporting the Democratic candidate, William Jennings Bryan, or splitting the prosilver vote by nominating someone else. Within a decade the Populists too had shuffled off the political stage.

The agrarian revolt petered out because farmers never organized successfully and because they never found the right issue around which to rally the faithful. Farmers remained divided among themselves by race, section, and interest. In the South their opponents used the race issue to keep white and black farmers from joining forces to become a formidable political presence. Northern farmers were distracted by party differences, policy splits (policies that might help wheat growers might not help other types of farmers), and the lack of a clear agenda or program around which to unite.

The currency issue could never provide such an agenda; it

was much too ephemeral, as comparison with the slavery issue makes clear. The slavery issue could not be addressed without making deep-rooted changes in the most basic American institutions; the currency issue could be dealt with merely by increasing the money supply. This in fact happened after 1896 with the discovery of gold in Alaska. A year later the depression of the 1890s ended and a period of prosperity marked by rising prices commenced. No more was heard of the silver issue until the Great Depression of the 1930s. The farmer's situation improved for reasons having little to do with politics. Rising prices and demand ushered in a brief golden age for farmers from the turn of the century to World War I.

Neither currency reform, railroad regulation, control of middlemen, nor any other farm issues lay at the heart of the farmer's problem. He was a businessman operating in an environment more favorable to other types of activity. The farm entrepreneur could not put together new structures or systems to exploit economies of scale in the same way as his industrial counterpart. He could not control costs or prices or most of the crucial elements in his production process. To a great extent he was a prisoner of a changing economy generating forces that were revamping the rules of the game by which he had always played. Too often he worsened matters by playing the game with a boom-or-bust mentality, borrowing heavily to expand when times were flush and leaving himself vulnerable to the inevitable downturn.

Technology remained the farmer's ally in the fight to increase productivity. After 1900 the gasoline-powered tractor, a vast improvement over earlier steam-driven models, proved invaluable in a wide variety of chores from plowing to pumping water to running other machines. By replacing animals it allowed land once used for feed to be used for human food crops. Cheap, versatile, and easy to maintain, the tractor became as indispensable to the farmer as the Model T Ford did to the general public. No single invention did more to ease the chores of farm life.

The future of the farmer, like that of other Americans, lay in organization, but not in the broad, loose form that characterized the protest movements of the late nineteenth century. In time farming too succumbed to the corporate lure; after 1900 the old family farm increasingly gave way to large agricultural enterprises that were often corporations. These organizations joined to create their own pressure groups such as the American Farm Bureau Federation, the National Farmers Union, and others, which brought them far greater gains than the diffuse political movements of the nineteenth century ever brought to small farmers.

Gradually farmers learned, as did labor, that the secret to success in the corporate economy was to support smaller but powerful pressure groups that could target specific goals rather than broad social reforms. Larger, more successful farmers learned this lesson first, just as they learned how government at all levels could be utilized to their own advantage. The lessons of the organizational revolution came slow to rural America, but they did come.

# 5

# The Corporate Society

> But just as ... a community realizes the conditions
> which all civilized communities are striving for, and
> advances in the scale of material progress ... so does
> poverty take a darker aspect. Some get a better and
> easier living but others find it hard to get a living at
> all. ... It is as though an immense wedge were being
> forced, not underneath society, but through society.
> Those who are above the point of separation are
> elevated, but those who are below are crushed
> down. ... This association of poverty with progress is
> the great enigma of our times.
>
> —Henry George,
> *Progress and Poverty* (1879)

THE CORPORATE SOCIETY arose in response to the
forces and needs of the corporate economy. As the organizational revolution spread through the social system, it influenced nearly every aspect of human activity. Things that had
been done on a casual, informal basis came increasingly to
be formalized and organized, whether at work, at play, or
even at home. To complicate matters, this change took place
just as American society was growing more complex and
diverse, thanks to an unprecedented wave of immigration.

This social change happened in large part because of the
unique nature of the corporation. It could apply vast re-

sources and an efficient organization to a specific purpose for an indefinite length of time. No individual could do this, and no public institution possessed the same drive or single-minded focus. Corporations also had two other features that awed and alarmed people. First, by allowing a company to grow to sizes never before imagined, they dehumanized its inner relationships. "A great business is really too big to be human," complained Henry Ford. "It grows so large as to supplant the personality of the man. In a big business the employer, like the employee, is lost in the mass."

Second, the larger a corporation grew, the more people puzzled over its inner nature and the effects it had on their lives. A popular phrase of the era betrayed this uneasiness by complaining that a corporation had neither a soul to damn nor a body to kick. Nor did it have a conscience to prick. Ambrose Bierce, in his delightfully mordant *Devil's Diction-ary*, defined a corporation as "An ingenious device for obtaining individual profit without individual responsibil-ity." In transcending human limitations, it seemed also to have transcended human restraints.

To most people the corporation was some new and imper-sonal creature. It was created and managed by men, but it was something more than men. Ironies abounded in its presence. Conceived as a servant of individual ambitions, corporations grew so spectacularly as to reshape those ambi-tions in unforeseen ways. Men pursuing their personal visions had created organizational monsters that threatened to destroy the open system that had spawned them.

It was the open system itself, which Americans had always prized as the heart of their civilization, that created this irony. Americans had gone to great lengths to concen-trate economic power and decision-making in the private sector. The point of the free enterprise system, after all, was to maximize the ability of individuals to pursue their interests with minimum legal or governmental restraints. But this philosophy had an unintended consequence: it divorced economic power from social responsibility. "The plain fact is," noted the social critic Herbert Croly in 1909, "that the individual in freely and energetically pursuing his own private purposes has not been the inevitable public benefactor assumed by the traditional American interpretation of democracy."

Within legal limits (and the law itself was often an ambiguous set of boundaries) people were free to amass as much wealth and property as they could in whatever manner they chose. They could do whatever they pleased with it and let the broader consequences fall where they may. In theory the ultimate restraint on a person's behavior was his own conscience, tempered and shaped by the values of religion and community. But the corporation had no conscience; although its values reflected those of its managers, they were by no means the same values held personally by those managers.

For these reasons no one knew exactly how to define or deal with corporations. They were a kind of mutant, with qualities unlike those of individual enterprises, operating in a system geared to the maximizing of individual freedom. How to fit corporations into this framework? The tendency of Americans has always been to cushion change by fitting new things into some familiar form; that is why the railroad came to be known early as the "iron horse" and the automobile as the "horseless carriage." The logical way to wedge the corporation into prevailing ideology was to define it as an individual in the eyes of the law, which is precisely what the Supreme Court did in a series of cases beginning in 1873.

This approach entitled corporations to the same protection given individuals under the Fourteenth Amendment. It also allowed the Court to duck the harder task of confronting the unique nature of the corporation and its sweeping influence upon American society. But the Court faced a genuine dilemma: to have ruled otherwise would have forced the justices to revise much of what Americans had long held sacred in regard to property rights and the proper role of government in economic matters.

Legal status as individuals gave corporations a great range of freedom. The result was a rapid development of corporate power and organization within the individualist framework, and a concentration of economic power that shocked many Americans. The total net assets of the Standard Oil empire reached $72 million in 1883, then soared to $143 million in 1895 and $359 million in 1906. Inflation did not produce this growth; the years 1865–1897 were the longest unbroken era of *deflation* in our history. Between 1873 and 1890 Andrew Carnegie and his partners earned $40 million in profits; by 1900 the company's *annual* profits totaled $40 million.

A survey of American industrial firms found 278 companies in 1917 with assets of $20 million or more. The list did not include transportation, utility, or communications companies. A survey of railroad systems in 1917 found 27 with assets exceeding $200 million; four had assets of more than $1 billion, led by the Pennsylvania Railroad with nearly $2.7 billion. The assets of electric power companies that same year approached $3.6 billion, of telephone companies $1.4 billion, and of telegraph companies $363 million. The Bell telephone companies alone boasted assets of $1.06 billion.

The largest enterprises dwarfed most other institutions. In 1891 the Pennsylvania Railroad employed about 110,000 people compared with 95,440 for the United States Post Office and 39,492 for the armed forces. By 1917 the number of civilian federal employees had reached 438,500, but the Bell telephone companies alone had 192,364 workers. In

1893 the federal government spent $388 million, collected $386 million, and had a national debt of $997 million. That same year the Pennsylvania Railroad alone spent $96 million, collected $135 million, and had a funded debt of $842 million. All the nation's railroads combined spent $732 million in operating expenses alone, collected $1.05 billion in revenues, and had $4.8 billion in funded debt.

This enormous concentration of economic power, and the political muscle it exerted at every level of government, threw the entire social system out of balance. Only once before, during the secession crisis, had so many Americans feared for the future of the Republic. Traditional attitudes of optimism and faith in progress found themselves swimming against a dark new undertow of pessimism and despair, a fear that society was changing too fast, hurtling down an unknown path toward an uncertain destiny. Thus arose cries of alarm that would be alternately echoed and shouted down through the next century.

Above all, Americans feared that the new corporate giants would shut down the open system and its traditional avenues to success. Much of the rhetoric of the Progressive movement that swept the nation during the 1900s complained that the new economic giantism was burying the little man. The promise of American life had always been rooted in the wide field of opportunities offered ambitious individuals; without an open system, critics warned, the whole scaffolding of democracy might collapse.

Gradually the political leaders of the era, sensing how deeply it ran in the public mind, picked up this theme and hammered away at it. "Our country—this great Republic—means nothing unless it means the triumph of a real democracy," thundered Theodore Roosevelt in 1910, "the triumph of popular government, and in the long run, of an economic system under which each man shall be guaranteed the opportunity to show the best that is in him.... In every wise struggle for human betterment one of the main objects, and often the only object, has been to achieve in large measure equality of opportunity." Two years later Woodrow Wilson, in his presidential campaign against Roosevelt, put the case even more vigorously:

> And this is the country... where no man is supposed to be under any limitation except the limitations of his character and of his mind; where there is supposed to be no distinction of class, no distinction of social status, but where men win or lose on their merits.... American industry is not free, as once it was free; American enterprise is not free; the man with only a little capital is finding it harder to get into the field, more and more impossible to compete with the big fellow. Why? Because the laws of this country do not prevent the strong from crushing the weak... and because the strong have crushed the weak the strong dominate the industry and the economic life of this country.

This sentiment rang true to many Americans. Men might strive for high place within a great business organization, but starting their own business proved much tougher going. The corporate economy encouraged people not to carve out a place for themselves but to find a niche within the existing scheme of things. Small businessmen, who found themselves locked into a perpetual struggle for survival, groped for a way to fight the vast, impersonal companies that squeezed them in so many ways. One could fight a tyrant or a competitor, but how was he or she to resist the oppression of a system? "The truth is," declared Wilson, "we are all caught in a great economic system which is heartless."

Even the fabulous wealth produced by industrialization after the Civil War seemed a mixed blessing because it was distributed so unevenly. The ethic of individualism and the concept of private property guaranteed people full possession of whatever fortune they could amass as a just reward for their initiative. But no one ever dreamed the fortunes would be so huge. While the material lot of society as a whole improved steadily, the gaps between classes widened into chasms. There had always been people with money in America, but never so many of them with so much of it. The age of enterprise created as a by-product a new and powerful aristocracy of wealth, which was soon converted into social status as well.

While the rich got richer, the ranks of the poor swelled into an army of misery. The stark contrast between wealth and poverty demolished the myth of America as a classless society and gave rise to a dark vision of one divided into a ruling plutocracy above and a demoralized working class below. Between them lay the fast-growing middle class, bewildered and intimidated by the rapid changes around them. Social novelists like Jack London (*The Iron Heel*) and Ignatius Donnelly (*Caesar's Column*) wrote grim prophecies of a bloody class war looming in America's future.

This same concentration of economic power also perverted the political system. "Liberty produces wealth, and wealth destroys liberty," warned reformer Henry Demarest Lloyd, who grasped the essential forces of his age even if he oversimplified their effects. Corruption and scandal tarnished every level of government, especially in the cities where political machines became a symbol for the evils infecting American democracy. In downtown America political office was a negotiable asset, but politicians elsewhere also bought votes and sold favors to whomever could pay for them.

State legislators wallowed in bribery, boodling, and back-scratching, and the sewer of corruption backed up into the lofty chambers of national government. Congress had always been the nation's longest-standing joke, but in the industrial era a steady procession of scandals soured laughter into despair and cynicism. Here too wealth made its power felt as men parlayed their fortunes into political office. So many wealthy men bought their way into the Senate that it became known as the "Millionaires' Club." While critics differed widely over remedies, they agreed upon one primary source of evil: the growing political influence of corporations and business interests.

Society itself was badly strained by the runaway momentum of industrialization. As the pace of change accelerated it could not help but disrupt traditional habits, values, and institutions. Americans had always embraced change as a sure sign of progress, but the amount and velocity of it in the industrial era simply overwhelmed them. A new fear arose that was to linger deep into the next century: somehow they were losing control of their lives and their destinies.

Sheer physical growth did much to unsettle the social order. Across the continent wilderness mushroomed into villages, villages into towns, towns into cities, and cities into sprawling metropolises. Rural folk, displaced by farm machinery that enabled fewer people to produce more food, flocked to towns and cities in search of opportunity and adventure. There they collided with waves of immigrants from abroad who were equally bewildered by the strangeness of their surroundings. The size of this migration was staggering. Between 1850 and 1920 the world's population increased about 55 percent while that of the United States jumped 357 percent. During these years 31.7 million people migrated to the United States, 14.5 million of them after 1900. By 1920 more than a third of the nation's people were either foreign born or had at least one foreign-born parent.

Apart from their numbers, these newcomers were more

foreign than ever. Before the Civil War almost 90 percent of all immigrants came from Great Britain, Ireland, and Germany. Their ethnic stocks, languages, and cultures were similar or at least familiar to most Americans. After the war, however, the proportion of newcomers from these places dropped to 63 percent in the 1880s and only 14 percent in the 1910s. In their place came people from Italy, Poland, Russia, and the Baltic states, which together made up more than 41 percent of the immigrants entering this country between 1890 and 1920.

These newcomers brought with them strange cultures and customs that did not assimilate easily into the mainstream of American life. They were slower to grasp and appreciate American traditions, spoke alien tongues, and harbored ideas some Americans considered dangerous. Their presence aroused dark fears and emotions that triggered a revival of "us and them" nativism. "The typical immigrant," thundered Congregationalist minister Josiah Strong in 1885, "is a European peasant, whose horizon has been narrow, whose moral and religious training has been meager or false, and whose ideas of life are low. Not a few belong to the pauper and criminal class."

In small town and city alike, many old-stock Americans recoiled at the influx of foreigners into what they deemed their private domain, and resented being jostled aside by a rapidly changing ethnic mix. The most vocal among them warned that the alien ideas and customs of the newcomers threatened the supremacy of the white Anglo-Saxon Protestant culture that had long dominated American civilization, and of which they were the proud custodians. Strong was but one of the voices bewailing the menace hanging over what the title of his book proclaimed as "Our Country."

The changes were real enough to raise the question of whose country it was. The United States had always been a nation of culturally, ethnically, racially, and religiously diverse peoples. Before the Civil War, however, the ethnic and cultural mix was scattered across the landscape, most black Americans were held in slavery, and the ethnic mix itself was not as diverse as it later became. After the war the slaves were free, the West was filling up rapidly with settlers, immigrants from strange lands were pouring into the country, and huge numbers of rural folk were flocking to towns and cities where they collided with newcomers from abroad. The mix had grown much larger, more diverse, and more explosive from being crowded together.

Society was becoming fragmented. The homogeneity and sense of community that had given preindustrial America some semblance of identity and cohesion was dissolving. In its place arose a social order tormented by extremes, dazed by the accelerating pace of change, and inflamed by tensions that often erupted into violence. This transformation did not occur overnight and certainly not everywhere at once. It came slowest to rural and small-town America, where people adhered to their old customs and life went on much as before with only an occasional hint of the storm raging beyond the horizon in the cities.

In grappling with these problems many Americans found that the old reliance on self-help was not enough. In the corporate economy, individual action could scarcely dent, let alone deflect, the course of action. The centers of economic power were large organizations; the sources of political corruption and social dislocation were organizations or forces too vast to be opposed and too complex to be understood. The conclusion was inescapable: if concerned individuals could not get at them directly or fight them alone, they must band together. From this realization flowed a massive surge toward organization that was the genesis of the corporate society.

This surge assumed many forms. Some groups organized to protect their private interests against the power wielded by corporate enterprise. These ranged from labor unions to business, farm, and professional organizations. A second type consisted of organizations to advance some broad public issue or attack a social problem. These covered a broad spectrum: reform groups, consumer leagues, charitable and philanthropic organizations, and organizations dedicated to fighting problems like alcoholism or child labor or prostitution. A third type arose for social, charitable, recreational, or cultural purposes: YMCAs and YWCAs, lodges, clubs, fraternal organizations, athletic teams, literary guilds, ladies' clubs, and many others.

Existing institutions were compelled to expand greatly to meet changing needs and new demands for services. The most obvious example was government, which began to grow at every level, but such institutions as schools and churches also responded to these pressures. Some organizations straddled these loose categories while others fell somewhere between them. What they all shared was the belief that only through organization could their voices be heard or their impact felt.

Here too businessmen led the way. Recognizing earlier than most people the need for new kinds of organizations to protect their interests, they devised an elaborate network of them. Once firms within an industry realized their common interests, they joined together in trade associations, first at the regional and then at the national level. Members exchanged technical and other information, and sometimes engaged in collusive pricing or other practices. Historian Thomas C. Cochran has estimated that a thousand of these organizations existed by the end of World War I, including the American Iron and Steel Association, the United States Brewers Association, the National Association of Stove Manufacturers, the National Association of Wool Manufacturers, and the National Millers Association.

Beyond the industry level, businessmen founded a variety of organizations to pursue larger interests. These included the National Chamber of Commerce, the National Association of Manufacturers, and the National Board of Trade, all of which began as local groups and evolved into state and then national organizations. Other groups formed to deal with specific issues: the Protective Tariff League, the American Anti-Boycott Association, and the American Manufacturers Export Association.

The size and strength of corporations, coupled with the rapid organization of business interests, forced workers to adopt the same tactic. Labor relations changed radically in the new corporate workplace as personal contact between owner and worker gave way to layers of salaried managers who derived their authority from distant sources. Managers tended to be concerned more with profit and efficiency than with human welfare. Their coming heralded the triumph of a market economy in which management-labor relations (the phrase itself was an invention of the era to describe a newly formalized relationship) were stripped of all social aspects, and labor was reduced to a commodity to be bought and sold.

Workers confronted not only a hierarchy of managers but a giant organization with which they could not bargain on equal terms. They accepted the going wage or went elsewhere, had no voice in their working conditions and no way to take a grievance to the owner. This loss of influence occurred just as many plants and factories were becoming hellholes in which to work. Increased use of machinery reduced skill levels and depressed wages, while the desire to cut costs gave rise to dreary, unhealthy, often dangerous workplaces. Numbed by fatigue, boredom, and long hours, workers often lapsed into carelessness and were maimed by the machines they tended.

Accurate data on crippling accidents in American industry before 1920 do not exist, but the impressionistic evidence suggests appalling numbers. By one estimate an average of 35,000 workers were killed and 536,000 injured every year during the period 1880–1900. Between 1905 and 1920 some 2,000 coal miners died every year in work-related mishaps. Those who survived faced another threat: loss of their job. A serious accident might cost the victim not only a limb or some fingers but often the ability to earn a living for self and family. The wave of immigrants pouring into cities created a labor surplus that kept wages down, as did the use of women and children in factory jobs. Age, sickness, insubordination, or simply the prejudice of a supervisor was enough to cost a person his job without warning.

Although real wages rose steadily between 1865 and 1920, the workday remained long. In 1890 it averaged ten hours for a six-day week; as late as 1920 skilled workers still put in 50.4 hours and unskilled workers 53.7 hours a week. That was when there was work; few laborers could count on having a job the whole year round, and uncertainty was never more than the next recession or depression away. A study by social reformer Robert Hunter in 1903 found unemployment to be the most common cause of poverty. "The annual wages of more than one workman in four," he noted, "suffered considerable decrease by reason of a period of enforced idleness."

Large numbers of workers struggled simply to keep afloat. "I didn't live, I simply existed," one woman told the New York State Factory Commission. "...It took me months and months to save up money to buy a dress or a pair of shoes." A reporter surveying one of the steel mill towns around Pittsburgh was struck by the appearance of the workers' children. "Their faces...are peculiarly aged in expression," he wrote, "and their eyes gleam with premature knowledge, which is the result of a daily struggle, not for life, but for existence."

In most cities workers were stuffed into ghettos of tenement houses that were sunless, airless, overcrowded, filthy, and reeking of garbage and excrement. Outsiders condemned them as breeding sties for disease, crime, despair, and degeneracy, but to some inhabitants they looked very different. One Jewish immigrant admitted,

> Even the slums of the days were beautiful to me compared to the living quarters of Lithuania...even though the toilet was in the hall, and the whole floor used it, yet it was a toilet. There was no such thing in Lithuania.... Here was running water. I saw horse cars and trolley cars, and when I saw a cable car on Broadway, I thought America was truly the land of opportunity.

The dominant characteristic of the American work force during this period was its incredible ethnic, racial, and cultural diversity, which made organization difficult. The growing number of women in the work force also complicated the mix; by 1920 more than 8.6 million women were holding jobs, more than 2.3 million of them in factories. Employers did not hesitate to play on ethnic and cultural differences to keep workers from organizing. Efforts by early unions to force concessions from management through strikes resulted in two decades of industrial strife that brought few gains and many losses to the workers.

"While workers remained divided by craft, nationality, and race," noted historian Melvyn Dubofsky, "employers united through mergers and trade associations." This imbalance of power impressed itself upon many workers with painful clarity. As one Pennsylvania coal miner put it:

The working people of this country suddenly find that their boasted republicanism is not able to save them from the miseries which they sought to escape. They find monopolies as strong as government itself. They find capital as rigid as absolute monarchy. They find their so-called independence a myth, and that their subjection to power is as complete as when their forefathers were a part and parcel of the baronial estate.

Gradually workers saw what their employers already knew: that organization might accomplish what they could not do by themselves. While unions had been around since the preindustrial era, they underwent a striking change in the industrial age. Some pursued a broad range of reforms that tried to render industrial capitalism more humane. The National Labor Union, founded in 1866, sought to give workers a voice in politics but collapsed in the depression after 1873. The Knights of Labor, which rose to prominence during the 1880s, hoped to enlist workers of all stripes in its struggle. "Our order contemplates a radical change in the existing industrial system," declared its general assembly in 1884, "and labors to bring about that change." But internal struggles and some rash strikes in 1886 shattered the Knights' fragile organization.

The decline of the Knights shifted leadership of the labor movement to the American Federation of Labor and its affiliated trade unions, which took a different approach to the struggle. Unlike the Knights, the AFL accepted the existence of industrial capitalism and worked within its constraints. Instead of advocating a wide range of social reforms in the belief that the workingman's lot could be bettered only by improving the social system, the trade unionists confined their agitation to bread-and-butter issues like wages, hours, and working conditions that directly affected members. Instead of engaging directly in politics, they operated as a pressure group seeking concessions from both major parties on the issues that mattered to them.

The triumph of trade unionism enrolled the labor movement as one more organized interest group in the corporate society. The era of turmoil, with its succession of bloody strikes that outraged public opinion, gradually gave way to one in which labor leaders joined with enlightened corporate managers to reform the workplace. "If your industrial organization cannot evolve some saner method of reconciling conflicting interests than twenty-four thousand strikes and lockouts in twenty years," proclaimed reformer and minister Walter Rauschenbusch, "it will be a confession of social impotence and moral bankruptcy."

Work stoppages still occurred, but unions fought to gain credibility and the legal right to collective bargaining. Although the latter did not come until 1935, the unions did compel employers in several major industries to deal with them. "I think capital should recognize organized and responsible labor," observed businessman and reformer George W. Perkins, "just as labor should recognize organized and responsible capital." What both sides recognized clearly was that the new corporate economy demanded not only organization but also order and continuity to be productive.

To achieve these goals many industrialists were willing to introduce a variety of employee reforms along with their new production techniques. Both sides had the same objective in mind: the creation of a harmonious work force that would produce at maximum efficiency under management's guidance. This was done, in Melvyn Dubofsky's words, by "improving illumination and ventilation, eliminating spatial obstacles to smooth production, maintaining better inventories of tools, and restricting the arbitrary authority of immediate shopfloor supervisors."

But social and industrial harmony eluded even the best of intentions. What suited large corporations did not always please smaller businessmen, who waged the old unremitting war against unionism. Predictably they organized into such groups as the National Association of Manufacturers, the Citizens' Industrial Alliance, and a number of regional and local organizations to combat the inroads of unions. Even so, union membership grew sharply, jumping from an estimated 447,000 in 1897 to nearly 2.1 million in 1904. The United Mine Workers alone soared from 14,000 members in 1897 to more than 300,000 by 1914.

As the larger unions grew they also became more corporate and bureaucratic. To protect their members' interests and keep others out, many unions concentrated ever more on weaving a tight web of formal work rules and procedures around their contracts. Union leaders donned suits and moved into headquarters buildings, where their life-styles came more to resemble those of the corporate leaders with whom they dealt than of the workers they represented. They did not bring harmony and order to the workplace. Improved organization enabled workers to strike on a grander and more coordinated scale. The number of strikes increased after 1900, violence still marred many of them, and the scale of major stoppages grew to impressive proportions. The corporate society had drawn the labor movement into its ranks, but the results proved quite different from what reformers had anticipated.

The rage for organization caught up the professions as well. This trend stemmed partly from the growing complexity and specialization of the industrial economy, which created new professions and demanded more of older ones. In preindustrial America, where versatility was highly prized, people moved easily from one occupation or profession to another because the process of entering them was so casual. None required extensive training, and few had rigorous standards of certification. A young man read law with a lawyer and then struck out on his own. Doctors might graduate from a medical school or simply apprentice or read up on the subject and hang out a shingle. Anyone who had graduated from college, and many who had not, could teach school.

Industrial society, with its rapid advance of technical knowledge and increased specialization, reversed the old pattern by emphasizing the importance of skills that could be acquired only through training or education. No ill-prepared doctor could absorb the rapid advances in medicine any more than a self-taught lawyer could master the intricacies of corporation law. As a result, professions and the training required to enter them grew more organized and systematized. The number of schools offering professional education jumped from 60 in 1850 to 283 in 1900, and their standards for graduation increased as well.

Every profession formalized standards for itself, then created an organization to formulate, monitor, and enforce them. Thus arose the American Medical Association, American Bar Association, American Association of University Professors, and many others. By 1920 virtually every profession, from educators to architects to social workers to musicians, had formed its own organization. Nor did the trend stop there. As each profession grew more specialized, the practitioners of these specialties formed their own organizations. Medicine spawned ten such societies between 1864 and 1888. "In the brief period of fifty years," declared the president of the AMA in 1883, "we have specialties for almost every part or region of the human body."

The American Association for the Advancement of Science, founded in 1848, gave rise to a large brood of specialized organizations such as the American Chemical Society

(1876), American Society of Chemical Engineers (1880), American Forestry Association (1882), American Ornithologists' Union (1883), American Society of Naturalists (1883), American Climatological Society (1884), American Institute of Electrical Engineers (1885), Geological Society of America (1888), National Statistical Association (1888), American Mathematical Society (1888), and American Physical Society (1888).

About two hundred learned societies sprang up during the 1870s and 1880s. As education became more specialized, scholars banded together in organizations around their disciplines. The American Social Science Association (1865) encouraged the creation of specialized organizations for modern language scholars (1883), historians (1884), economists (1885), church historians (1885), political scientists (1889), and even folklorists (1888). In the business world one of the most powerful organizations belonged to the bankers, whose American Bankers' Association arose from a foundation of forty-five state groups as well as numerous local clearing-houses.

The power and influence of these groups varied widely, as did the functions they performed. All enabled members to meet and exchange information; most worked actively to advance the interests of the profession. By establishing standards of training and conduct, many cast amateurs and fraudulent practitioners into disrepute. The setting of standards served two vital functions: it protected the public from charlatans, and it enabled many professions to set their own standards free from outside interference. The organization could then invest its members with the cloak of professional legitimacy and even limit the number of newcomers to prevent excessive competition.

Professional organizations also served as a badge of personal identity in an age when traditional forms of self-identity were crumbling. People in the corporate society tended to define themselves by their job; the old inquiry of "Who are you?" gave way to "What do you do?" As work of many kinds became more specialized, it acquired a mystique that spread quickly from the professions to other occupations and became a characteristic of the corporate society. The age of the specialist or "expert" had dawned. But expertise was a two-edged sword. On one side it helped identify people; on the other it separated people from one another. Experts had trouble talking about their work with anyone except their colleagues, which narrowed both their social and intellectual horizons. This added another element of instability to an already volatile social order.

All these groups—businessmen, wage earners, farmers, professional people—sensed in the corporate economy some threat to their well-being and took refuge in organization. The character of their organizations resembled the corporate model in being private entities created to serve the self-interest of their members. Most performed some public service or at least paid lip service to the ideal of public responsibility, but these usually took a back seat to their primary mission. In effect, the corporate society embodied the same fatal flaw of the corporate economy: the divorce of power from social responsibility. Like corporations, these interest groups tended to view the problems of the larger society through a prism colored by their own needs and values.

Those individuals concerned about the problems spawned by the transition to an industrial society found themselves powerless unless they too banded together. Confronted by poverty, slums, crime, waste of human and natural resources, environmental destruction, racial and ethnic strife, political corruption, and a vast array of other problems lumped together under the rubric of the "Social Question," reformers attacked them by creating an equally wide array of organizations: civic leagues, reform clubs, settlement houses, commissions, the Anti-Saloon League, Consumers' League, National Conservation Association, Federation of Good Government Clubs, National American Woman Suffrage Association, National Child Labor Committee, Municipal Voters' League, and hundreds more. These groups too tended to spring up at the local level and gravitate toward state and national organizations.

Nearly all these organizations were private groups seeking to deal with public problems. Government at every level also found itself under pressure to respond to the growing list of problems wrought by industrialization. Any such effort would mark a reversal of the traditional policy that maximized individual freedom by keeping governmental activities as minimal as possible. This policy of making decisions by drift and default had served the rise of the corporate economy well, but life in the corporate society had grown too complex to be left at the mercy of private interests with all their power. Something had to be done to restore balance, and the most logical action was an expansion of public power.

The assumption had always been that competition would regulate and preserve the market; instead it had spawned giant firms that threatened to dominate the market. Adam Smith's "invisible hand," long the cornerstone of the free-market system, gave way to the visible hand of organization and management in the modern business enterprise. "As the modern business enterprise acquired functions hitherto carried out by the market," observed Alfred D. Chandler, Jr., "it became the most powerful institution in the American economy and its managers the most influential group of economic decision-makers."

To match this power, government had little choice but to

fight size with size. New services and better delivery of old ones required more staff, more money, and an enlarged structure. Between 1880 and 1920 the federal government created the Interstate Commerce Commission, the Departments of Agriculture (raised to cabinet level in 1889), Commerce and Labor (created in 1903, divided into separate departments in 1913), Division of Forestry, Bureau of Corporations, Civil Service Commission, Federal Reserve Board, Federal Trade Commission, Federal Power Commission, Children's Bureau, and a myriad of special commissions to study particular problems.

At the same time existing agencies grew by taking on new responsibilities. In 1881 the federal government employed 100,200 civilians; that figure shot up to 239,476 by 1901 and 655,265 by 1920. With growth came a spiraling federal budget which leaped from $268 million in 1880 to $6.4 billion in 1920. For decades the federal government had supported itself chiefly from revenues produced by import duties; now it had to find new sources of income. In 1913 the Sixteenth Amendment to the Constitution, providing for a federal income tax, was ratified after years of bitter struggle over the issue.

This burst of growth sent the federal government down the road to bureaucratic giantism and an active role in many areas of American life formerly untouched by it. Passage of the Interstate Commerce Act in 1887 thrust it into the fateful task of regulating an industry for the first time. In 1890, the year after New Jersey passed its landmark statute legitimizing holding companies, Congress responded with the Sherman Antitrust Act. The transformation of the federal government from a small, passive institution into a large, active one was another major feature of the corporate society and one that followed the corporate model of growth from a small firm to a mammoth organization.

State and local governments went the same route. Most social problems surfaced at these levels and had to be confronted there first, usually by expanding the powers of government and extending the range of its services. But this growth did not come easily; at first state and local governments wilted before the mass of problems wrought by industrialization. A growing hostility toward abuses of power by state legislatures led to a movement between 1870 and 1900 to curb their powers. As economist Henry C. Adams lamented in 1887, "The corporations rose upon the ruins of the States as centers of industrial administration."

State legislatures found themselves caught in a maze of contradictory pressures. Citizens demanded more services and lower taxes, special interests craved their own private brand of pork, politicians increasingly viewed office as a source of power and profit, and reformers cried for an end to corruption and a wholesale attack on social evils. Historian Morton Keller has estimated that in the late nineteenth century states spent between 25 and 33 percent of their outlays on education, 20 to 25 percent on debt service, 15 to 20 percent for public welfare and protection, and less than 10 percent for economic development. State indebtedness fell 26 percent during the 1880s, which helped state budgets at the cost of skimping on social services just when the demand for them was growing rapidly.

Once the depression of the 1890s lifted, states with large urban populations especially felt strong pressure for social expenditures. These pressures inflamed the struggle for power between state and municipal governments. It is easy to forget that the city is legally another form of corporation deriving its charter from the state. By 1900 the nation had more than ten thousand incorporated cities and towns of all sizes, varying as widely in the powers they wielded as in their size and nature. Rapid industrial growth forced cities to regularize and professionalize services once left to volunteer groups. These changes required new sources of revenue and powers that could only be obtained by amending their charters.

This fight led to two distinct battles. On one front, cities fought to gain home rule from state legislatures; on another front, rival urban factions clashed over who should rule at home. State legislatures had seldom interfered in municipal affairs, but after 1850 they began to exercise a more active role. Most were dominated by rural interests who viewed cities with a mixture of suspicion and envy. Legal authority J. Allen Smith explained in 1907 why states were eager to extend their control over cities:

> The city offered a rich and tempting field for exploitation. It had offices, a large revenue, spent vast sums in public improvements, let valuable contracts of various kinds and had certain needs for water, light, rapid transit, etc., which could be made the pretext for granting franchises and other privileges on such terms as would insure large profits...at the expense of the general public. That the political machine in control of the state government should have yielded to the temptation to make a selfish use of its powers in this direction, is only what might have been expected.

In many states the legislature installed in cities a system of independent boards to administer such functions as education, utilities, water, and maintenance. As the board system spread to most major cities, it stripped city councils of their administrative functions and confined them to legislative duties. This separation of powers scattered real authority across a maze of officials and boards, thereby eroding the capacity of officials to govern and increasing opportunities for graft.

Legislatures wielded power over basic municipal services as well as taxing power, and could strip local officials of their authority at will. In 1901 the Pennsylvania legislature removed the mayor of Pittsburgh from office and directed the governor to appoint his successor; in 1885 the Massachusetts legislature placed the Boston police under state control. State party leaders routinely expanded their patronage by putting "friends" on city payrolls or specially created bureaus or commissions. Attempts to free cities from legislative control met a legal dead end in 1923, when the Supreme Court declared in its *Trenton v. New Jersey* decision:

> The city is a political subdivision of the state, created as a convenient agency for the exercise of such of the governmental powers of the state as may be entrusted to it.... The state may withhold, grant, or withdraw powers and privileges as it sees fit.... In the absence of state constitutional provisions safeguarding it to them, municipalities have no inherent right of self-government which is beyond the legislative control of the state.

In effect municipalities lacked real self-government. Their citizens could not determine tax rates, the uses to which their money would be put, their election procedures, educational system, public works priorities, or other basic functions. A city could not borrow money or raise revenue or feed beggars without applying to the state legislature for a special enabling act. Cleveland discovered in 1911 that its city council could not control the subsurface of public highways, provide public lectures and entertainments, require the isolation of tuberculosis patients, regulate the appearance of buildings that fronted on public highways, banish dogs, chickens, and other noise-making animals from the city, or manufacture ice for charitable distribution.

Thus arose the fight for home rule, which took many

forms between 1870 and 1920. Some reformers tried to persuade state legislatures to allow cities above a certain size the right to frame their own charters. Missouri was the first to adopt this approach in 1875, but by 1912 only eight other states had followed suit. Some states tried to classify their cities by size and then tailor legislation to fit each class; others tried to curb meddling by amending their constitution to ban special legislative acts having to do with cities. While curbing special acts eliminated some of the worst abuses, the first decades of the twentieth century found home rule still beyond the reach of most American cities.

Local government remained the black sheep of American democracy. The form of governance in cities varied so widely that the political scientist Frank J. Goodnow admitted, "We really have no system of city government." In 1891 a New York state senate committee itemized the confusion in blunt language:

> It is impossible for any one, either in private life or in public office, to tell what the exact business condition of any city is.... Municipal government is a mystery even to the experienced.... The conflict of authority is sometimes so great as to result in a complete or partial paralysis of the service.... Our cities have no real local autonomy.... Consequently so little interest is felt in matters of local business that in almost every city in the state it has fallen into the hands of professional politicians.... These are conditions which if applied to the business of any other corporation would make... successful administration as impossible as they are today in the government of our municipalities, and produce waste and mismanagement such as is now the distinguishing feature of municipal business as compared with that of private corporations.

The fight for home rule sometimes made unlikely allies of two groups fighting to rule at home: urban bosses and the reform elements who sought to oust them. Like other corporations, cities needed effective organizations to carry out their functions. Nowhere was order and system more urgently needed than in the large industrial cities with their swelling populations, crying need for basic services, and exploding social problems. The old ruling elites, who had once governed cities, abandoned their traditional civic roles and fled to the suburbs, leaving a vacuum of leadership.

In their place arose a new breed of men eager to make a business of politics. Like other businessmen, these political entrepreneurs possessed a talent for bringing order out of chaos and turning existing structural weaknesses to their own advantage. In the cities they forged political monopolies called machines, whose inner workings were no less disciplined and profitable than industrial corporations. What the trust and the holding company were to the economy, the political machine became to municipal government.

Cities could no longer be governed by the old model for the smaller township, which featured a homogeneous population and a ruling elite. When urban reformers and businessmen said they wanted good government, they usually meant a small, passive operation run on "sound business principles" with a low tax rate. But this model was no more suited to coping with the raw vitality of changing urban environments than was the township. Moreover, businessmen themselves had different needs. Some wanted franchises or contracts, others licenses or waivers or special regulations. Industrialists had one set of demands, bankers another, real estate developers and proprietors of small businesses still others.

The new urban bosses succeeded by applying the principles of the organizational revolution to the politics of the industrial city. Their machines flourished because they got things done when no one or nothing else could. They did this by transforming political power into a market commodity to be sold for profit to the highest bidder. "Politics is business," observed Lincoln Steffens, who probably knew more bosses personally than any man in America. "... The politician is a business man with a specialty." New York's Tammany Hall boss Richard Croker agreed. "Like a business man in business," he said affably, "... I work for my own pocket all the time."

Like the giant corporations, the political machine arose in response to disorder and instability and prospered by supplying vital services that were not being provided efficiently by existing institutions. To accomplish this it devised new mechanisms (district and ward organizations) for organizing raw materials (voters), production equipment (political office), and the market. For both business and political entrepreneurs, efficient organization held the key to success, and maintaining it was vital.

The power of political bosses in American cities was often exaggerated by those who failed to understand their role as businessmen. Most bosses acted as brokers for a diverse constituency of clients; they ruled not by force but by satisfying their customers' needs. They bought political power as cheaply as possible and sold it as dearly as possible. In the process they provided important social services to the cities at a time when no one else was providing them. Most of the urban reformers who mounted campaigns to oust these bosses never grasped the important functions performed by them for the lower classes of the city who provided the votes to keep the machine in power.

The surge of urban reform after 1900 took many forms, most of them aimed at replacing the boss and his corrupt machine with new types of organizations, such as the city commission and city manager systems, designed to provide efficient, honest government. Some reformers called for the replacement of old-line politicians with trained specialists and experts. Nearly all these reforms fell short of expectations, and few coped successfully with the immense array of social problems that plagued the industrial city.

Once the dimensions of these problems overwhelmed state and municipal authorities, they sought help from Washington. This was a logical course since many of the industrial society's stickiest problems transcended state boundaries: railroad regulation, antitrust restrictions, factory working conditions, child labor, social welfare issues, pure food and drugs, and environmental issues, to name but a few.

In the industrial era, then, all roads led to organization. As the contours of the corporate society gradually emerged from the fog of social dislocation, they revealed a new skyline of expectations and realities. It became clear that power could be obtained only through organization, and that those who organized effectively did far better than those who did not. The tighter the organization, the narrower its aims, and the greater the resources at its command, the more likely it was to achieve its purpose. Individualism remained the most prized virtue of our folklore, but in reality the individual had become less a prime mover and more a part of some greater whole, a cog in social machinery that was growing larger and more elaborate.

Since private power could be organized far more easily and efficiently than public power in the American framework, it remained the chief instrument of purpose despite mounting complaints that government was poking its nose into everything. Corporations, lobbies, political machines, and other private interests used their superior resources, efficiency of organization, and clear sense of focus to gain power at the expense of consumers, workers, reformers, and the disorganized mass of people like the poor who lacked comparable resources and often disagreed over what they wanted and how to get it.

Skilled workers organized far more effectively than un-skilled ones; the best farm organizations belonged to the large agricultural interests, not the dirt farmers; doctors and lawyers defended their interests far better than teachers. Government could command vast resources but lacked unity of purpose or direction. Too often it was made to serve the will of private interests powerful enough to get what they wanted from it. In that sense, at least, the public sector still functioned largely as an adjunct of the private sector.

The pattern of the future was clear: the corporate society would remain a private society. The vision of a balanced society in which power was shared to some degree by all the groups within it continued to hover in the distance like a mirage. Real power remained firmly in the hands of private interest groups reluctant to accept or acknowledge responsi-bility for the broader social consequences of their actions.

# 6

# The New American Landscape

> The modern city marks an epoch in our civilization.
> Through it, a new society has been created. Life in
> all its relations has been altered.... The modern city
> marks a revolution—a revolution in industry, poli-
> tics, society, and life itself. Its coming has destroyed
> a rural society, whose making has occupied man-
> kind since the fall of Rome. It has erased many of
> our most laborious achievements and turned to
> scrap many of our established ideas. Man has en-
> tered on an urban age. He has become a communal
> being.
>
> —Frederick C. Howe,
> *The City: The Hope of Democracy* (1905)

IN THIS OBSERVATION the reformer Frederick Howe
captured an essential feature of the new American landscape. Not only did cities transform the texture and values of
American life, they also triggered a deep and enduring
cultural clash between city dwellers and rural folk. While
this division had long been present in American society, it
grew more bitter as cities expanded in number, size, and
importance. The farm and village dominated preindustrial
America, endowing it with a cluster of values and beliefs;
after 1850 the city challenged that position with its own
strikingly different values and beliefs.

Urban America was the central stage on which the great drama of industrialization was played out. The corporate economy was born and nurtured in the industrial city along with nearly all the social problems related to industrialization. The effort to deal with these problems brought much of the corporate society into being. In turning to organization as a way to stabilize their volatile environment, urban dwellers created a new social system with the city as its nerve center.

Industrialization tilted the demography of the nation toward the cities. As noted earlier, the population more than tripled between 1850 and 1920; it shifted from rural to urban areas at an even faster rate. Most of the flood of immigrants poured into cities, but even more people flocked there from the country. In 1850 the United States had 237 urban places (defined as 2,500 or more people) with 15 percent of the total population. Most of these were small towns and villages; 174 of them had fewer than 5,000 people. The nation had only ten cities with 50,000 or more people, one with half a million inhabitants, and none with a million.

By 1920 those figures had jumped to 2,722 urban places with more than 51 percent of the population. There were 144 cities with 50,000 or more people and 5 with more than a million. The number of places with 5,000 or fewer people increased to 1,970, but many of these were suburban satellites to cities rather than rural communities. During these seventy years the urban population grew at an average rate of about 48 percent each decade, twice that of the whole population.

This shift of population toward cities also signaled major changes in the way people earned a living, as farming took a back seat to nonagricultural pursuits. In 1850 between 55 and 64 percent of Americans made their living from the soil; by 1920 that figure had dropped to about 26 percent. This triggered another change with profound consequences. In 1820, according to one estimate, about 80 percent of Americans owned the property from which they made a living, which meant they were self-employed. By 1940 that figure had shriveled to 20 percent; the other 80 percent worked for someone else and depended on wages or salaries for support.

Other figures indicate that as early as 1870 a majority of the labor force worked for someone else. The trend was obvious: economic opportunity in the industrial society lay less in going one's own way than in finding a place within the existing scheme of things. "For them [the middle class], as for wage-workers," concluded sociologist C. Wright Mills, writing in the 1950s, "America has become a nation of employees for whom independent property is out of range. Labor markets, not control of property, determine their chances to receive income, exercise power, enjoy prestige, learn and use skills."

The work force swelled not only because the population grew but also because a larger proportion of it went to work—39 percent in 1920 compared with 34 percent in 1850. Women accounted for part of this change; in 1920 they made up more than 20 percent of the work force compared with 15 percent in 1870. These figures underscore the fact that the new technologies of industrial America created more jobs than they replaced. The organizational revolution brought into being a mass of new jobs within corporate and other bureaucratic structures. These new employees, who became known as "white collar" workers to distinguish them from "blue collar" factory workers, emerged as the backbone of a new middle class that became the fastest growing group in the nation.

The new middle class was overwhelmingly urban. Its growth reflected an economy in which every component was becoming increasingly specialized, thereby creating new functions that had to be serviced by people with new skills or more sophisticated versions of old ones. Where the old middle class had been confined mostly to business and professional people, the new middle class included a variety of managerial, technical, clerical, sales, and public service workers. Their ranks quadrupled between 1870 and 1910. White-collar workers alone increased from 374,433 in 1870 to 3.2 million in 1910, and comprised more than a third of the entire middle class.

During that same period the number of professional people jumped 366 percent, and the variety of professions expanded almost as much. The number of teachers and professors soared from 128,265 to 614,905; of reporters and editors from 5,375 to 34,382; of designers and draftsmen from 1,291 to 47,449; of artists from 4,120 to 34,094, and of musicians from 16,170 to 139,310. Between 1870 and 1900 the ranks of trained nurses increased 110 percent, veterinarians 80 percent, and technical engineers 60 percent.

"Success in the middle class," noted historian Burton J. Bledstein, "increasingly depended upon providing a service based on a skill, elevating the status of one's occupation by referring to it as a profession." New fields of expertise emerged. By 1910 more than 39,000 people called themselves accountants, a profession that did not even exist in 1870. The American Association of Public Accountants was formed in 1887 but had only thirty-five members and no employees by 1892. Four years later New York became the first state to pass a law certifying public accountants.

In 1905 the association merged with another organization to create a truly national association of professional accountants. By 1914 some thirty-three states had passed laws certifying public accountants; by then charges were already being hurled in certain states, notably New York and Illinois, that accountants unfairly restricted access to the profession by imposing unreasonable admission standards. Undaunted, the association continued to press for strict standards, rules of conduct, and the formal education of accountants.

Other occupations followed this same course. Undertakers formed a national association, adopted a code of ethics in 1884, and heeded the advice of the association president that the key to respectability was to "get the public to *receive us as professional men*." By the 1890s the term "mortician" dignified the profession, and courses in "mortuary science" entered college curriculums. Plumbers too got the message. One practitioner explained to the American Public Health Association in 1891 that "Plumbing is no longer merely a trade. Its importance and value in relation to health, and its requirements regarding scientific knowledge, have elevated it to a profession."

This expansion of professions and practitioners reflected an economy that was not only more specialized but also wealthy enough to funnel more resources into education, the arts, leisure, and recreation. Professional athletes came into being as sports grew more formalized and turned into businesses. The first professional baseball team appeared in 1869; seven years later the National League was formed. College football became a craze as its rules were formalized during the 1870s. The first All-American team was named in 1889; four years later Harvard hired its first paid athletic coordinator. New technologies like the camera, the phonograph, and the motion picture spawned whole industries staffed by professions that had never before existed.

Managers and technicians, more than any other groups, heralded the emergence of a maturing corporate economy. Managers are the officer corps of bureaucracy whose ranks multiply when institutions expand in size and complexity and must then break down into more specialized units.

Technicians are the offspring of advancing technology as it becomes too sophisticated to be entrusted to people not formally trained for the task. Technical progress itself creates a hierarchy of specialists as discovery, invention, and innovation grow more institutionalized.

Lewis Corey has estimated that the number of managers soared from 121,380 in 1870 to 893,867 in 1910. Of this latter figure, about 65 percent worked in manufacturing, transportation, communications, mining, and construction firms, 5 percent in trade, and 6 percent in banking. By 1910 the field had also grown varied enough to be carved into upper (39 percent) and lower (61 percent) management. The number of technicians increased from 8,118 in 1870 to 109,198 in 1910. Of the latter number, 81 percent were engineers who had separated into specialized fields (civil, electrical, chemical, mechanical). The others included chemists, metallurgists, assayers, and laboratory technicians.

White-collar workers were the foot soldiers of the corporate economy: bookkeepers, clerks, secretaries, typists, sales people, drummers, sales agents, telephone and telegraph operators, and many more. These jobs required less training and education than the professions or other middle-class occupations and were therefore accessible to people from the working class who regarded them as a step upward from the drudgery and squalor of the factory. Although the hours were often long and the pay meager, they offered more cheerful surroundings, a measure of prestige, greater security, less exhausting toil, and the hope of advancement.

In the corporate society higher education took on a new importance as the training ground for the professions and occupations. The road to success ran directly through the rapidly growing educational system. As one Harvard student said frankly in the 1870s, "The degree of Harvard College is worth money to me in Chicago." Higher education served two conflicting purposes in the corporate society. It show-cased the democratic system by offering a pathway to success to anyone who could meet its requirements and was willing to work hard. At the same time it produced corps of "experts" in many fields and professions whose formal training and status enabled them to shut out others seeking entry to the field. The result was a uniquely American creation that might be called an authoritarian meritocracy.

The mushrooming of the middle class reflected the coming of a new social as well as economic order. It was a vertical order centered increasingly on contact with people on the ladder of one's own profession and less with people in the horizontal world of daily life. Burton Bledstein explained the change this way:

> In the later nineteenth century, for instance, an instructor in a college might earn less income than a policeman, but the wide difference in the status of their occupations precluded any common or class sympathy. Whatever their means, the professor and the policeman socially lived worlds apart, and their mistrust of each other in the everyday world—the horizontal one—was mutual.... Looking vertically, middle-class Americans lacked a corporate sense of community.

In this way American society was becoming as vertical as its new city landscapes. It was also growing more segmented. As urban dwellers the new middle class possessed a much greater variety of life-styles, values, and interests than country folk, and their access to the widening stream of new, cheap goods available in cities made them more keenly aware of material things. Americans had always defined status to a large extent in terms of wealth, and in the socially fluid world of the city wealth expressed itself in terms of possessions and their display. Surging productivity helped give rise to a new epoch of material civilization at a time when the inhabitants of cities, who were mostly strangers to one another, needed ways to define their identity to others.

The goods were there thanks to a revolution in methods of distribution and retailing as well as production. In 1850 the distribution of goods was dominated by wholesalers on the eastern seaboard. Several layers of middlemen separated producers of goods from consumers, and there was little order or clear relationship among these layers. Most retailers were independent operators who catered to local markets. Firms tended to specialize in either wholesaling or retailing but not both. Urban shops usually specialized in particular lines of goods while the country store, which dominated rural America, carried everything in sight.

The coming of the railroad and the telegraph rendered this system obsolete by enabling mass producers of goods to reach distant markets. The emergence of Chicago as a rail center fostered the shift in control over consumer goods distribution from the east coast to the Midwest, forcing Eastern wholesalers to flood the West with salesmen and catalogs in an effort to hold the trade.

Wholesalers who had once handled goods on commission turned into jobbers who owned the goods they sold. While wresting control of distribution from middlemen on the east coast, they forged large buying networks to obtain goods directly from manufacturers, and marketing organizations through which to sell to general stores in the country and retail shops in the cities. These techniques were extended to the whole range of consumer goods: clothing, furnishings, hardware, drugs, groceries, jewelry, watches, furs, tobacco, liquor, boots and shoes, leather products, furniture, wood products, stationery, china, glassware, and paint and varnish.

Jobbers replaced a cumbersome, localized distribution system with one that could handle a large volume business by dealing direct with manufacturers on one side and retailers on the other. To do this they relied on an army of salesmen or "drummers" who scoured the countryside to sell goods and bring back vital market information. They also needed an efficient purchasing organization, which consisted of scattered buying offices and buyers who worked out of the home office and quickly became the most important figures in the larger jobbing houses.

This new system of distribution led to the rise of giant mercantile firms like Marshall Field, which jumped from $9.1 million sales (of which $1.5 million was retail) in 1865 to $36.4 million ($12.5 million retail) in 1900. As early as 1870 A. T. Stewart in New York, the nation's largest dry goods dealer, did $50 million in sales ($8 million retail) and employed two thousand people. Similar firms were springing up throughout the country, ending Eastern dominance of the distribution business. Sheer growth turned these companies into large organizations with departments performing specialized functions like shipping, accounting, and credit.

Impressive as this system was, it soon faced stiff competition from two newer kinds of enterprise. On one side giant retailers began to buy direct from manufacturers and sell direct to consumers, thereby eliminating the jobber; on the other side some manufacturers began forging their own wholesale marketing and distribution networks and purchasing agencies. The result was yet another radical change in the distribution and marketing of consumer goods.

Retailers marched into the wholesale realm by the same process of steady, sometimes spectacular growth. "Mass retailers," observed Alfred Chandler, "began to replace wholesalers as soon as they were able to exploit a market as large as that covered by the wholesalers." By building their own purchasing organizations, the retailers could buy direct from manufacturers and generate an enormous sales volume.

They also had the advantage of direct contact with consumers. Three new forms of retailer appeared on the scene: the department store, the mail-order house, and the chain store. Each one followed in a different way the same road to profits through high volume of sales, low margins, economies of scale, and a rapid turnover of stock.

The department stores first appeared in the 1860s and catered to the surging urban market. Some of the great founders, like Marshall Field and A. T. Stewart, came to retailing from wholesaling; others, like Rowland Macy and John Wanamaker, started in retail clothing or dry goods and expanded by adding new lines of goods. The giants in the field thrived on a blend of centralization and diversity. Within one huge building they carried a broad variety of goods organized around separate departments, thereby providing consumers "one-stop" shopping. Success was often measured in the ability of each department to outsell the city's leading specialty shop in that line of goods.

To achieve high volume the department stores pioneered a number of techniques that have since become standard practice. Stewart originated the one-price rule, and Wanamaker carried it to new heights. The old method of haggling over the price of every item was eliminated in favor of a set price. Wanamaker also backed every purchase with a full money-back guarantee which allowed the return of merchandise for exchange or cash. To move goods during slow periods like January and August, Wanamaker created special sales.

Wanamaker also advertised more extensively and originally than anyone had before, often writing the copy himself. Everything he did was designed to keep the stock turning. "We must move the goods," he exhorted. "If one of your salesmen sees an article around, unsold, until he gets tired of looking at it, how can you expect to find—ever—a satisfied purchaser for it?"

The great department stores celebrated their success by erecting huge emporiums, and Wanamaker was no exception. In 1911 he opened a gigantic new store in Philadelphia, twelve stories high with three more underground and occupying a whole city block. The largest building in the world devoted to retail merchandising, it housed a striking succession of display areas, courts, halls, and galleries with a grand court in the center topped by a dome rising 150 feet atop marble arches. One gallery featured the largest organ in the world; two other organs resided in the Greek and Egyptian halls, the latter flanked by winged figures and stolid Sphinx heads. "Surely," quipped Wanamaker, "we are well organized."

Just as imposing new railroad stations like Grand Central and Pennsylvania in New York became spectacular gateways to visitors, so did the grand department stores become the city's cathedrals of commerce. The same could not be said for the mail-order houses; their enormous influence was felt more in the country than in the city. Even more than department stores, the mail-order houses owed their existence to the presence of a rail and telegraph network coupled with innovations in the mail system such as a special rate for catalogs in 1873, the establishment of rural free delivery in the 1890s, and the addition of parcel post service in 1912.

For decades the general store had the rural market to itself, the only alternative being a long trek to the nearest town to buy goods and haul them back. After the Civil War a number of merchants began selling such items as tea, jewelry, and books by mail. In 1872 Aaron Montgomery Ward formed a company with his brother-in-law to market a variety of goods out of Chicago through mail-order catalogs. By the late 1880s Montgomery Ward reached a nationwide market with a 540-page catalog listing more than 24,000 items. No one challenged its supremacy until the 1890s, when a former watch salesman named Richard W. Sears bought out his timid partner, Alvah C. Roebuck, and took in two new ones, Aaron Nusbaum and Julius Rosenwald. From this new combination arose the dominant retailing firm in the nation.

Based in Chicago, Sears, Roebuck added new lines of goods to its mail-order business until it had twenty-four merchandise departments by 1899. Thanks in part to the newly created rural free delivery, sales exploded from $745,000 in 1895 to $37.8 million in 1905, leaving Montgomery Ward in its wake. By 1915 sales reached a staggering $106.2 million and then more than doubled to $245.4 million in 1920.

The secret to the company's success lay in the creation of an efficient organization and in its catalog, a masterpiece of sales propaganda crafted with loving care by Sears himself. Drawing on his sure grasp of the rural mind, Sears described his wares in cheerful, homespun prose, invited the folks to visit his Chicago plant, and hammered home his policies of low prices, high quality, and guaranteed satisfaction or money refunded without question. "Sears was in love with his catalog," noted business historian Richard S. Tedlow, "and no moonstruck lover ever studied his mistress's habits with greater care and concentration." So popular did the catalog become that in 1897 Sears put 318,000 copies into circulation; by 1908 that figure had jumped to nearly 6.6 million.

To succeed, Sears had to overcome formidable obstacles. He was asking farmers, who were always short of cash and slow to part with it, to buy goods sight unseen from strangers in a distant city. Unlike the general store, which charged high prices and extended credit to strapped farmers at high interest rates, Sears kept prices low with a cash-only policy buttressed by his money-back guarantee. By blanketing farm magazines with ads for his catalog, Sears hoped to break down buyer resistance and make Sears, Roebuck a household name in rural America. No one spent more lavishly on advertising than Sears; his outlays climbed from $400,000 in 1898 to $3.5 million by 1908.

No catalog, however alluring, could long stay in business unless it delivered on its promises. Here too Sears pursued the relentless goal of selling the highest-quality goods at the lowest possible prices. As the company historians put it: "Sears guaranteed his $11.96 cookstove to cook. It cooked. And it cooked for years and years. Sears's plows would plow, and Sears's washing machines would wash. That was what farm families wanted; and that was what they got from Sears, Roebuck."

Sewing machines provide a classic example of how Sears operated on his belief that "the strongest argument for the average customer was a sensationally low price." In 1897 he priced Sears sewing machines at $15.55 to $17.55 when national brands sold at three to six times that amount. That fall he cut the $16.55 model to $13.50 and was deluged with orders. Happily he browbeat his supplier to lower his price by a dollar so Sears could drop his price to $12.50; in one month he received nineteen thousand orders. By 1900 the same machine was selling for $7.65. So too with cream separators, an invaluable implement to farm families. Sears took his $62.50 model, which already sold for a third less than competitors, and turned it into three models selling at $27, $35, and $39.50. The product became a sales leader.

So well did Sears accomplish his goal that the rush of business nearly overwhelmed his company. The biggest task then became forging an organization capable of handling the flood of orders generated by the catalog. By 1908, when Sears retired, the company had become a mammoth organization that was integrating backward to control the supply of key products. It owned all or part of sixteen manufacturing plants (the number would pass thirty by 1918) and in 1920 extended its retailing operation by opening stores in major cities to gain a share of the mushrooming urban market. Where the department stores, with their high-volume, low-price efficiency, dealt a severe blow to local specialty shops, Sears devastated rural retailers and the wholesalers who serviced them.

Chain stores made little impact until the 1900s, but in two decades they forged a pattern of retailing that still prevails. They tended to specialize in goods not yet dominated by the big mass retailers—groceries, drugs, furniture, shoes, cigars—or in a broad line of smaller items that made them a variety store. Working within the same framework as other mass retailers, they put the pieces of the commercial puzzle together in slightly different ways. Most bought in quantity direct from manufacturers and relied on a high volume of sales at low prices and a fast turnover of stock. They tended to locate in small towns or on the fringes of cities, and did a regional rather than a national business.

The dramatic changes wrought by chain stores can be seen clearly in the area of food retailing. Most food stores were small, inefficient shops that operated on the basis of high profit margins and low turnover. In 1878 a bright young man named George Huntington Hartford, who had begun as a clerk, took over the management of the Great Atlantic & Pacific Tea Company (A & P), which had been selling tea since 1862. Hartford decided first to increase the volume of tea sales by opening more stores (the company had about two hundred by 1901), and then went a step further by expanding the line of goods carried. "We first got into baking powder and then into extracts," recalled John A. Hartford, George's son, who followed him in the family business. "... We got into the grocery business gradually."

Even more than his father, John believed money could be made by selling in volume at low prices. In 1913 A & P began opening a new line of what it called "Economy Stores." A company officer explained the distinction this way:

> In our so-called "Economy Stores" we do not make any deliveries, we have no telephone communications, we close the store when the manager goes to lunch, we sell strictly for cash, we give no premiums, trading stamps or other inducements. In our regular stores we do give trading stamps, we do make deliveries, we have telephones, in some instances we give credit.

Between 1914 and 1916 A & P opened a breathtaking 7,500 stores and soon closed half of them to eliminate the weakest. The Hartfords gave the stores the same basic appearance inside and out. By 1920 A & P had 4,600 stores earning a profit of $4.8 million on sales of $235.3 million. But that was only the beginning: by 1930 the company owned 15,700 stores earning profits of $35 million on sales of nearly $1.1 billion. It had become the fifth largest industrial corporation in the nation and by far the largest chain organization in the world, with sales that exceeded those of Sears, Montgomery Ward, and J. C. Penney combined by $173 million.

By 1890 at least half a dozen grocery chains were doing business in different parts of the country. Frank W. Woolworth pioneered the variety or "dime" store and was soon followed by S. H. Kress and S. S. Kresge. United Drug and United Cigar evolved into national chains, as did many of the variety stores. Like other mass retailers, the chains resorted to ruthless cost-cutting and paid the lowest possible wages. "We must have cheap help," explained Woolworth, "or we cannot sell cheap goods." But size and efficiency alone did not transform the process of distribution. As Chandler has emphasized, the key was speed—the ability to turn stock rapidly and to internalize a host of complex market transactions within one large enterprise.

These transformations had profound effects on both the economy and society. They organized and systematized two functions that had earlier been more casual, complex, and cumbersome. By creating national and regional markets, they fostered the rise of standardized products and the spread of brand names that could be marketed over wide areas of the country. They raised standards of quality and therefore customer expectations. In the long run they spurred the rise of a strange and wondrous new phenomenon, the consumer economy.

Industrialization changed not only what workers did and how they did it but also the places where it was done. People flocked to where the jobs were, and in the process created a new American landscape. Rural areas blossomed with towns, and cities gobbled up surrounding countryside as suburbs. Whole towns sprang up around a mill or steel plant or some other industry; Gary, Indiana, was created from scratch to house workers in a giant steel mill complex. This had been the pattern since the dawn of the industrial era, when mill villages dotted the landscape of New England. As one early observer described it,

> In 1840 it would have been difficult to find 50 out of 479 townships in Southern New England which did not have at least one manufacturing village clustered around a cotton or a woolen mill, an iron furnace, a chair factory or a carriage shop, or some other representative of the hundred miscellaneous branches of manufacturing which

had grown up in haphazard fashion in every part of these three states.

The pattern intensified as industrial cities grew larger, more numerous, and more specialized. The result was not merely growth but a new kind of urban environment with strikingly different economic, political, and social relationships. Industrial cities attracted an amazing diversity of peoples who streamed into them seeking work or excitement or a start on the road to fame and fortune. In these turbulent environs bristling with energy, immigrants found jobs, middle-class people status and a rising standard of living, and the upper class a perfect arena in which to amass wealth and define their superiority through the gaudy display of a lavish life-style.

Some cities, like Birmingham and Duluth, grew because they stood near the site of raw materials or sources of power; others, like Atlanta, lay on key transportation lines or markets. Still others had favorable climates, land, or labor costs. When small factories blossomed into large plants, subsidiary businesses moved to town to service them. Transportation and distribution facilities expanded, banks opened, and armies of workers moved there in search of jobs. A growing population needed grocers, butchers, merchants, mechanics, barbers, doctors, druggists, ministers, teachers, craftsmen, saloonkeepers, and dozens of other tradesmen. The construction industry boomed, requiring still more labor.

In many industrial towns the primary industry was the sun around which the rest of the local economy revolved. If it was prosperous, so were they; if it slumped, the depression extended to them. The degree of specialization or dependence was often startling. In 1900 no less than 90 percent of the wage earners in South Omaha, Nebraska, and 73 percent of those in Kansas City worked in the meat industry; 89 percent of those in McKeesport, Pennsylvania, toiled in iron and steel; 86 percent of those in Bethel, Connecticut, made fur hats; 81 percent of those in Tarentum, Pennsylvania, relied on the glass industry; 77 percent of the workers in Brockton, Massachusetts, made boots and shoes.

Some cities became renowned for one product. In 1900 Troy, New York, made 85 percent of the nation's collars and cuffs, while 64 percent of all oysters came from Baltimore. Connellsville, Pennsylvania, produced 48 percent of the nation's coke; Waterbury, Connecticut, 48 percent of its brassware. Nearly 46 percent of all rugs and carpets were made in Philadelphia, 39 percent of gloves in (where else?) Gloversville, New York, and 27 percent of jewelry in Providence, Rhode Island. In all, nearly two-thirds of the nation's primary industrial activity in 1900 took place in its 209 cities with populations of twenty thousand or more.

Here, then, were the ingredients of the new American landscape: many more people than ever before from a vastly more diverse mix of cultures, thrown together in closer proximity to perform a much more complex variety of jobs in cities and towns that were themselves growing and changing at a rapid pace. The new industrial city had become for many the engine of progress, and technology was the fuel that made it go. The historian David Potter once observed that "More Americans have changed their status by moving to the city than have done so by moving to the frontier." These migrants did more than change their status; they changed the tenor of American life itself.

# 7

# Technology Triumphant

> Until about 1865 the voltaic battery, which gener-
> ated electricity by chemical decomposition, was prac-
> tically the only means for producing electricity for
> industrial and commercial purposes. It was through
> its agency that the telegraph, the electric light, and
> many other discoveries in electricity were made....
> But with the advent of the dynamo electricity has
> taken a new and very much larger place in the
> commercial activities of the world. It runs and
> warms our cars, it furnishes our light, it plates our
> metals, it runs our elevators, it electrocutes our
> criminals; and a thousand other things it performs
> for us with secrecy and dispatch in its silent and
> forceful way.
>
> —Edward W. Byrn,
> *The Progress of Invention* (1900)

IN 1849 AN American inventor named Walter Hunt
spent three hours fiddling with a little device that received
patent number 6281. He later sold for $400 the rights to
what became known as the safety pin. Two years earlier
Richard Hoe, the son of an inventor, took out a patent on
what became the prototype for a rotary press that could
print two thousand four-page newspapers in an hour, or
twice the amount of a cylinder press. By 1852 a larger,

improved model could turn out ten thousand complete papers an hour, but even that was not enough. As newspapers grew larger and readers more voracious for news, other innovations followed until Henry A. Wise Wood devised a giant press in 1917 that could churn out 240,000 *eight*-page papers every hour.

These stories capsule two key aspects of the American experience with technology: the ability to create devices that were useful, and then to make them steadily better, faster, and more versatile. The American knack for invention has been around from the beginning, but during the industrial era it reached unprecedented heights of output and achievement. "No other nation," wrote Thomas P. Hughes, "has displayed such inventive power and produced such brilliantly original inventors as the United States during the half century beginning around 1870." It was, Hughes predicted, an epoch of achievement that would be equated with the Renaissance in Italy, the age of Louis XIV in France, and the Victorian era in England.

Like politics and art, the term "technology" means different things to different people. Hughes defined it broadly as "the *effort* to organize the world for problem solving so that goods and services can be invented, developed, produced, and used." From another angle it is an effort devised by inventors and put to practical use by entrepreneurs, without whom the greatest of devices would languish in obscurity. The United States was blessed with an abundance of both types, and their presence in turn owed much to a continent teeming with natural resources and the opportunity to exploit them with minimum interference from government.

As noted earlier, an abundance of natural resources alone does not insure rapid economic development or industrialization. David Potter explains what else was required for these to happen:

The working economic assets of a society depend not only upon the supply of natural resources but also upon the effectiveness with which resources are converted into energy or productive capacity or goods.... This effectiveness in the conversion of resources is not a matter of largesse or luck. It is determined by the economic organization and the technological advancement of any given society, and these factors are the result of human endeavor and achievement.

Technology was the engine that drove the process of industrialization, and the accelerator that sped up its cycles of change. Like most other activities of the period, it was shaped and influenced by the organizational revolution until it became as institutionalized as other areas of American life. In 1850 invention rested in the hands of men who were often quirky loners, some of whom were lionized as cultural heroes. By 1920, though individual genius still drew headlines, most invention and innovation had passed into the hands of research laboratories sponsored by corporations or other agencies. What had once been a casual, individual process evolved into systems of mammoth size conducted through elaborate bureaucratic procedures.

"Inventors, industrial scientists, engineers, and system builders," emphasized Hughes, "have been the makers of modern America." Above all else, they implanted in American culture a pattern of constant, accelerating change that impressed people deeply enough to become their definition for progress. One new machine spawned a dozen others as well as a series of improved versions of itself. The resulting stream of innovations reached deep into the fabric of American life, affecting every detail of daily life from cooking and other chores to reading to bathing.

These changes did not come easily or without cost. While technology itself is value neutral, its effects on society are value laden and often devastating. Progress proved a bumpy road because every new technology had to beat out competing ones and threatened entrenched interests with extinction. The coming of the automobile doomed the makers of carriages, wheels, and buggy whips, while the spread of indoor plumbing turned the chamber pot into a museum piece. The ability of railroads to cross rivers via bridges wiped out the thriving transfer and ferry trade at every crossing. Ready-made shirts sent the collar and cuff industry into oblivion.

Older industries and trades withered away and were replaced by new ones, bringing loss of jobs and identity to some people and gain of both to others. Craftsmen and artisans saw the skills of a lifetime obliterated by machines that performed the same tasks with greater precision at immensely faster speeds. Displacement became a way of life in American society as mobility had always been, and together these forces reinforced the adage that in the United States nothing ever stayed the same for very long. The credo of most Americans was that the future would surely be better than the present, and technology was the tool that would make it so.

The key to this process lay not merely in the steady stream of technological innovations but in a revolution in the sources of power that made the machines go. "It is a social fact of incalculable importance," stressed David Potter, "that between 1820 and 1930, by exploiting new sources of power, America increased forty fold the supply of energy which it could command per capita."

The sheer dimensions of this change boggle the mind. Between 1870 and 1920 American consumption of energy jumped about 440 percent. In 1870 wood accounted for about 73 percent of all energy used, with coal supplying almost all the rest. By 1920 wood provided less than 8 percent of energy used, coal soared to 73 percent, oil contributed 12 percent, and natural gas 4 percent. More important, the ways in which power was used shifted dramatically. A growing portion of energy was being funneled into the production of a new source of power that was itself giving birth to a whole new generation of technology.

Electricity burst onto the scene so swiftly that in little more than a generation it came to dominate the age. The pattern of its development offers a prime example of nearly all the forces that shaped the industrial age. Faith in its future had been around longer than most people realize. "The belief is a growing one," noted Commissioner of Patents Thomas Ewbank in 1849, "that electricity in one or more of its manifestations is ordained to effect the mightiest revolutions in human affairs." The success of the telegraph helped inspire that prediction, but electricity languished for decades because no one could figure out how to generate it in large quantities and transmit it safely over long distances. Until those problems were solved, products needing more than small amounts were not likely to succeed.

The dynamo solved the first of these problems. It used an external force, like a steam engine, to move an electric conductor in a magnetic field, which produced a current in the conductor. By the 1870s dynamos had been built that could provide large amounts of current at low cost. These new machines launched a new era by making electric power available cheaply and in quantity; no longer did users have to rely on batteries, which were cumbersome and limited in their output.

At first many people thought electricity would become a magical new primary source of energy, replacing other sources like coal and wood. It soon became clear, however, that since its production required coal, oil, or some other form of energy, electricity's primary function was to *transmit* power from the source to places of use faster, cheaper, and more conveniently. Electric lines sent power where it had never gone before and eliminated the labyrinth of cables, belts, and shafts formerly needed to move power to and within places.

Work on the dynamo provided insights for the development of an electric motor. Indeed, the motor was at bottom a dynamo running in reverse: it passed a current through an electrical conductor in a magnetic field to create a force acting on the conductor, which could then be used to power something else. By 1880 researchers understood that this type of motor would be crucial in transmitting electric power, and that the motor could draw its own power from the dynamo just as electric lights did. To become commercially viable, electricity needed efficient, reliable dynamos and motors along with some sort of network to connect them.

Even before this happened, inventors were busy developing products using electricity. During the 1870s arc lights emerged as the first successful form of electric lighting. In 1878 the innovative John Wanamaker installed a series of arc lights in his department store. One amazed observer described the display as "twenty miniature moons on carbon points held captive in glass globes." Two years later, when the town of Wabash, Indiana, boldly replaced its gas street lamps with arc lights, crowds of people came to witness the event. "Men fell on their knees," reported one spectator, "groans were uttered at the sight, and many were dumb with amazement."

Stores and factories bought the new lights, and Cleveland led a parade of cities that began installing arc lights in place of gas lamps. Huge arc lamps were fitted about the capitol dome in Washington, and the new Brooklyn Bridge sparkled with arc lights when it opened in 1883. The trend posed an ominous threat to gas companies, of which there were more than four hundred in the United States by 1875, but there was no going back. Arc lights became standard street lighting for many years and were also used as ship lights, beacons in lighthouses, searchlights, and even stage lights.

Arc lights had two major limitations, however, that prevented their use for house or interior illumination. They were extremely bright, and their intensity could not be reduced. Moreover, they burned a substance composed chiefly of carbon. These drawbacks spurred other inventors to develop a form of electric light without these limitations. Two technical problems were especially formidable: finding a filament of a high-resistance substance that would glow with white heat but not be consumed, and discovering a way to utilize electric current for a single lamp as well as a series at the same time.

The story of Thomas A. Edison's struggle to solve these mysteries has become part of American folklore, but he was only one of many inventors grappling with the problem. Edison patented his celebrated version of the incandescent lamp (or what became known as the light bulb) in 1880, but he needed the help of others to win the race. No electric lamp would be feasible if it had no other source of power than batteries, and no lamp using filaments at high heat could function without the protection of a vacuum. The dynamo solved the first problem, and the invention of a mercury vacuum pump by Herman Sprengel in 1865 eliminated the second one.

On this foundation Edison forged brilliant solutions to the many problems posed by incandescent lamps. He devised one that was cheap and durable. Each light could be controlled separately and turned on and off like gas. To power his new lights, Edison had to design a new type of dynamo. To demonstrate its feasibility he formed a company to build a power station in New York City on Pearl Street near the financial district. The opening of the Pearl Street station in 1882 launched the electrical age, but not quite in the direction it would eventually take.

Pearl Street gave the world its first system for distributing electrical power, not only for light but for fans, printing presses, and heaters that were all driven by electric motors. Some small towns like Appleton, Wisconsin, and Elgin, Illinois, adopted the new system, but its basic flaw soon became apparent. Edison relied on direct current, which had technical limitations that drove costs up sharply when power had to be carried any distance. Another system, developed by George Westinghouse, used alternating current which allowed the flow to switch from high to low voltage through use of a device called a transformer. This enabled current to flow long distances over high-voltage lines and then be lowered to safe levels at the user source.

Although alternating current had its own technical problems, Westinghouse pushed vigorously to solve them. Edison clung stubbornly to his direct-current system in which he and his supporters had a huge investment. He used every weapon at his disposal to ruin Westinghouse in what became known as the "War of the Currents." In the end Edison lost because he proved as wrong on this issue as he had been right about the light bulb. Alternating current became the standard for lighting and later for use in electric motors as well.

As the technology of electricity was improved and refined, new uses were found for it. Improved motors permitted use of the power in factories, where it spurred a dramatic increase in output. The development of steam turbines lowered the cost of producing electricity and enabled factories to buy power more cheaply from central power stations than from small local plants. Urban transportation was transformed by street railways, overhead trolleys, and subways. These uses, coupled with an increased reliance on electric lights for commercial and residential use, gave rise to an electrical utility industry, which assumed giant proportions by the 1920s. In 1902 there were already 2,250 plants generating electricity in the nation; by 1920 the number had jumped to 3,381. During that time the consumer's cost per kilowatt hour dropped from 16.2 cents to 7.5 cents.

Besides electric utility companies, large manufacturing firms arose to serve the growing demand for electrical supplies and products. Three companies came early to dominate the manufacture of electrical equipment: Edison General Electric, Thomson-Houston, and Westinghouse. In 1892 the first two firms merged into a new giant, General Electric. During the explosive growth of the coming years, the industry remained under the control of these two major companies.

Here, then, was a major industry where none had existed before, spurred to rapid growth by a steady procession of technological innovations, organized and integrated in a remarkably short time, and providing a new form of energy that was destined to revolutionize American life in ways not even its most enthusiastic advocates could imagine. From its use flowed lighting in all its many forms, streetcars, subways, automobiles, thermostats, elevators, machines for factory and office, motion pictures, phonographs, radios, and the whole catalog of household appliances that would transform the American home.

Electricity was but one force feeding the enormous growth in productivity after 1880. Where the coming of mass distribution owed more to organizational innovations, the rise of mass production was more the offspring of new technologies. Besides using energy more intensively in ways made possible by electricity, production relied on more efficient machinery and equipment and raw materials of higher quality. New machines, though expensive, improved efficiency at every stage by producing far more with fewer workers and integrating the process in ways never before possible.

A classic example occurred in the tobacco industry, where a machine patented in 1881 by James Bonsack could turn out 70,000 cigarettes in ten hours. Within a few years improved versions increased output to 120,000 a day; by contrast a skilled worker could produce 3,000 at best. James B. Duke was the first American to adopt the machine and quickly dominated the industry, adding other machines to make packages and fill them with cigarettes automatically. In 1881 four firms combined to produce a new machine capable of making billions of matches and packing them in boxes. Their Diamond Match Company seized the world match trade in short order and held it for decades.

During the 1880s, too, Procter & Gamble took charge of the soap industry by using a new mechanical crusher to produce its Ivory brand in huge quantities. George Eastman perfected a continuous process for making photographic negatives and later a box camera he called the Kodak. These products made his firm's name synonymous with film and photography. Flour milling became centered in Minneapolis, where Charles Pillsbury built an empire by packaging his flour and selling it under his own name instead of the old-fashioned way in bulk.

New machines enabled Henry P. Crowell to create an integrated mill that turned out crushed oats in astronomical quantities. To generate a market for his newfangled oatmeal, Crowell packaged it as Quaker Oats and advertised it nationally, much like Ivory soap was promoted. His effort gave rise to the breakfast cereal, which was as strange then to Americans as prerolled cigarettes. Other manufacturers such as Borden, H. J. Heinz, Campbell Soup, and Libby used continuous-process canning techniques to turn out food products that changed American cooking and eating habits.

By 1900 alert businessmen grasped the pattern that was unfolding. Continuous technological innovation led to dramatic increases in output. The revolution in methods of distribution, coupled with the new transportation and communications networks, allowed products to be marketed on a national scale. In fact, it demanded a revolution in marketing as well. To produce in quantity made no sense unless one could sell in quantity, and this could best be done by giving products a brand name that would identify them to consumers across the nation. A brand name could also be advertised on a national scale.

No product demonstrated the power of a brand name more spectacularly than Coca-Cola. Here was a product that was in no way a necessity, could be consumed in a variety of places, had plenty of substitute products, and existed to satisfy only a fleeting urge: thirst. Yet Asa Griggs Candler and his successors managed to transform this drink into a hugely profitable business and ultimately a national icon as well. A Supreme Court decision in December 1920, which established Coca-Cola's trademark as inviolable in a suit brought by the company against the rival Koke Company of America, produced this revealing opinion from Justice Oliver Wendell Holmes, Jr.:

> Since 1900 the sales have increased at a very great rate corresponding to a like increase in advertising. The name now characterizes a beverage to be had at almost any soda fountain. It means a single thing coming from a single source, and well known to the community. It hardly would be too much to say that the drink characterizes the name as much as the name the drink.

Soda water had been around the United States since the 1800s, and received a boost in the 1830s when the first patents were issued for soda fountain machinery. Flavored syrups were added to soda water and dispensed in bottles or on draft. The first trademark names for soft drinks were not registered until the 1870s: Lemon's Superior Sparkling Ginger Ale in 1871, Hires Root Beer in 1876, and Cliquot Club beverages in 1881. Even at these late dates the market for carbonated water flavored with syrup had not been clearly defined. Like mineral water, these drinks were regarded more for their alleged curative powers than anything else.

Coca-Cola was invented in May 1886 by an Atlanta druggist, John Styth Pemberton, who sold his interest in it the next year for $283.29. Candler bought complete ownership of the company in 1891 for $2,300; in 1919 his sons sold that same stock to a consortium headed by Ernest Woodruff for $25 million. By then Coca-Cola sales had reached $24.3 million with profits of $4.6 million, and its meteoric rise had barely begun. Few companies have ever risen from such modest, unpromising origins to dominate, indeed define, a market so completely.

Pemberton's great discovery was the formula for a syrup that made a delicious drink when mixed with carbonated water. Candler took this product and, with missionary zeal, spread it across the map of the United States. The object, declared an officer later, was "to make it impossible for the consumer to *escape* Coca-Cola." Since thirst was a transitory state that could be as easily satisfied by one product as another, it was essential to make Coca-Cola omnipresent. The consumer had not only to like the drink; he or she had to have immediate and convenient access to it.

To create product recognition Candler spent huge sums on advertising—not only in newspapers, magazines, and billboards but also on matchbooks, calendars, doilies, baseball scorecards, pencils, blotters, window signs, and dozens more such items. He also created a large and talented sales force that specialized in face-to-face contact. The salesmen did more than talk; they listened well too, picking up vital market information, and they went everywhere. No store or site was too small for Coca-Cola. By 1920 its product was being handled by 1,871 jobbers, and 78,375 soda fountains.

Another quantum leap was made after 1900 when Coca-Cola developed a network of bottlers who mixed the syrup with carbonated water, like the fountains, but then bottled it and shipped the drink to the outlying region. "I wanted to bring Coca-Cola to the country people outside the limits of the fountain," explained Joseph A. Biedenharn, the man who became the first bottler in 1894. Candler never warmed to the idea, which had to await widespread acceptance of the Crown Cork and Seal bottle cap, a device invented in 1892. By 1920, however, Coca-Cola served 1,095 bottling plants, and the drink could be taken anywhere people wanted it.

From this pattern flowed an entirely new specie of economic order: the consumer economy. Brand names invaded one product area after another, converting local markets into national ones. By replacing local and regional items with national, prepackaged ones, they standardized not only goods but tastes as well. In a single generation, observed the historian Bernard Weisberger, "the country moved from a homemade to a store-bought society." And the store itself kept changing, moving from the general store or specialty shop to department stores, mail-order houses, and chain stores, all of which relied on their own name as a kind of brand in itself.

Technology helped this process along in ways that went beyond production. At Sears, for example, rapid growth created organizational problems of nightmare proportions.

To handle the tidal wave of incoming orders required not only new systems of organization but also machines and devices to automate scheduling and shipping. A paragraph in the company's 1905 catalog described proudly the progress that had been made:

> Miles of railroad tracks run lengthwise through, in and around this building for the receiving, moving and forwarding of merchandise; elevators, mechanical conveyors, endless chains, moving sidewalks, gravity chutes, apparatus and conveyors, pneumatic tubes and every known mechanical appliance for reducing labor, for the working out of economy and dispatch is to be utilized here in our great Works.

Technology also reshaped the office and the ways it did things. The telegraph and telephone sped the flow of information, and the growth of companies increased the amount of paperwork needed to keep track of everything. Tabulating or adding machines made bookkeeping easier and more accurate. Versions of the best-known office appliance, the typewriter, had been around the United States since 1829, but none went into widespread office use until the 1880s when the Remington typewriter became popular. The advent of carbon paper provided the first cheap and easy method of making copies.

The telephone and the typewriter transformed the office in yet another way: they opened the door to female employees in what had been an all-male bastion. E. W. Byrn enthused in 1900 that the typewriter had "established a distinct avocation especially adapted to the deftness and skill of women, who as bread winners at the end of the Nineteenth Century are working out a destiny and place in the business activities of life unthought of a hundred years ago."

No sector of the economy escaped the impact of new

technology. Sewing machines transformed the garment, boot and shoe, and a dozen related industries. A host of innovation in the metals field lifted those industries to new heights through the use of intensive heat and electrochemical processes. One such improvement shrank the cost of aluminum from $12 per pound in 1878 to 33 cents in 1900. New machines coupled with imaginative plant designs resulted in dramatic increases in efficiency. One such wonder of the industrial age rose in Pittsburgh, where Alexander Holley designed an enormous integrated steel plant for Andrew Carnegie.

Agriculture too entered a new era as reapers, binders, threshers, harvesters, cultivators, and other machines sent productivity soaring and cut the amount of labor needed. Centrifugal milk skimmers, incubators, and other devices made farm chores easier. Advances in canning technology increased the market for agricultural products and spurred the development of new machines like the Sprague corn cutter, which could slice enough corn off cobs in one day to fill fifteen thousand cans. The Scott and Chisholm pea sheller removed as many peas from pods as six hundred workers could do by hand. A small device called the "iron chink" could process seventy or eighty salmon a minute for canning. One area of the food industry after another moved toward a continuous-process method of production.

Refrigeration, especially for railroad cars, made possible the rise of huge industries in meat packing, fruits, and vegetables. As late as 1900 the Imperial Valley of California was a barren plain without a single inhabitant; a decade later it had become one of the richest agricultural regions in the nation, sending endless trainloads of produce eastward. Chicago emerged as the center of a vast meat-processing complex where efficient factories butchered and dressed livestock for shipment by rail to every corner of the nation along with an impressive array of by-products.

It was truly said that these giant meat plants took hogs and used everything but the squeal. Besides the pork, the lungs, heart, liver, and trimmings went into sausage, the feet were pickled or made into glue, the intestines stripped and turned into sausage casings, the softer parts of the head made into a type of cheese, the fat rendered into lard, the bristles used for brushes or upholstery stuffing, the blood put into albumen for photographic uses, meat extracts, and fertilizer, and the bones ground for fertilizer. Even the water in the tanks where the hogs were boiled was concentrated and used in fertilizer or extracts.

The rise of a food industry radically altered the eating habits of Americans. Canned foods grew immensely popular for their convenience and ability to provide seasonal foods all year round. The production of bread, butter, and cheese as well as meat moved from the farm to the factory, and milk moved to cities in whole trainloads. Store-bought bread was not as tasty as a homemade loaf, but it was quicker, easier, and cheap. Here was another instance of technology speeding up the pace of life for a people already notorious for zooming through meals at a pace deemed barbaric by many Europeans.

Americans also dressed better as the steady mechanization of the clothing and shoe industries brought store-bought apparel into the reach of most people. By 1900 most men and about half of women and children wore clothes produced in factories. Styles once reserved for the wealthy, whose clothes were made to order, could be copied and sold in quantity. Foreign visitors remarked how hard it was to tell the clerk from the banker or the shopgirl from the society matron by their dress. Social optimists spoke glowingly of a classless society wrought by the democratizing of style. That never happened, but the speed and volume of mass production in clothing and shoes did feed the emerging consumer economy by encouraging faster, more frequent changes of style.

New technology changed American homes as well, not only their furnishings but also how they were built. Improved tools combined with new techniques to speed up even the oldest of construction jobs. Steam-powered shovels made short work of foundations, and the invention of a concrete mixer in 1900 made possible the widespread use of concrete. That same year a machine for finishing floors was introduced. The pneumatic drill appeared in 1890, and carpentry moved from hand to mill work, enabling scroll designs for windows and doors to become commonplace. The house itself became more of a factory product as early versions of prefabricated homes appeared before 1900. Ready-mix paints and varnishes also became standard factory items, and their application was made easier with the invention of spray guns.

Inside the home the most dramatic improvement came from central heating, in which forced steam heat circulating through the house via pipes replaced the fireplace or stove. As early as 1874 William Baldwin gave the world its first radiator, but the new device did not gain widespread use until cast-iron models were developed in the 1890s. Indoor plumbing and septic systems greatly improved sanitation for those fortunate enough to have them. Water quality improved thanks to techniques developed by several American engineers. A whole new industry arose to manufacture sinks, bathtubs, and toilets made of enamel. The bathroom, a room new to most American homes, emerged as a showcase of new technology.

No place displayed the impact of change wrought by new technology in more varied or dramatic forms than the city.

As the nerve centers of industrial society, cities did more than grow; they changed size and shape constantly, putting ever more distance between them and rural America. The city was one giant construction site where something was always going up or coming down to be replaced by something else. Only in the United States did buildings seem to have a shorter life span than people as new technologies and changing usages rendered them obsolete in their original form.

An outpouring of technological innovations made possible this pattern of constant change. Structural steel, new foundation techniques, plate glass, electricity, elevators, fireproofing, plumbing, and new communications devices permitted the construction of entirely different kinds of buildings. The most conspicuous product of these innovations was the skyscraper, a new kind of building that soared upward on a framework of steel. "In the skyscraper," marveled a British architect, "America has invented and developed a wholly new and revolutionary form and type of building that is absolutely and characteristically her own."

The skyscraper was a triumph of technology. Its skeleton of steel girders, every leg anchored in its own foundation, used walls not for support but merely to keep out the weather. The development of plate glass provided windows capable of resisting wind and pressure, while the use of hollow tiles for floor arches offered excellent insulation and fireproofing at much lighter weight than other masonry. The upper floors could not have been reached without the brainchild of Elisha Otis. His newfangled elevators were driven first by hand, then by steam and later electricity.

In its own way the skyscraper became a visual symbol for the new industrial age, starting at modest levels and soaring upward to undreamed of heights. The first steel-frame version, William Le Baron Jenney's Home Insurance Company Building in Chicago, was built in 1885 and rose a modest ten stories. At first New York resisted the new technology. When the eleven-story Tower Building, the city's first steel-framed structure, was completed in 1889, it attracted so few tenants that architect Bradford Gilbert resorted to putting his own office on the top floor to reassure people that it was safe.

New York actually imposed a five-floor limitation on buildings in the interest of public health and safety, but this restriction soon vanished in a frenzy of construction. The American Surety Building (1895) reached twenty stories, the St. Paul Building (1896) twenty-six, and the Park Row Building (1898) thirty-two. All these monuments were overshadowed by architect Cass Gilbert's crowning masterpiece, the Woolworth Towers, with its fifty-five floors soaring 760 feet into the air. At its opening in 1913 President Woodrow Wilson pressed a button that illuminated eighty thousand electric lights in the building. It soon acquired the epithet "Cathedral of Commerce," a fitting monument to the man who had built a far-flung empire of dime stores and unabashedly craved a structure that would command international attention.

That same year New Yorkers reveled in the opening of another monument to modern progress, Grand Central Station. Large cities competed vigorously with each other in the building of both skyscrapers and transportation temples which served as the gateway to the city, and none outdid Grand Central for the daring and ingenuity of both its architecture and engineering. It featured two separate levels to segregate suburban from interurban traffic, a loop enabling trains to turn around without reverse movement, complete electrification, and a system allowing trains to move in either direction on all four approach tracks.

The skyscrapers and rail terminals were no more impressive monuments to technology than the new bridges crossing the rivers along which every major city was built. Imposing new spans like the double-decked suspension bridge above Niagara Falls (1855), the Eads Bridge in St. Louis (1873), which was the first to cross the Mississippi River, and the magnificent Brooklyn Bridge (1883) eliminated water barriers to growth by allowing traffic to flow in and out of cities with ease. This encouraged the rise of "bedroom suburbs" that gave cities an enlarged population during the day and pushed their boundaries outward into the surrounding countryside.

Improvements in mass transit also expanded the physical limits of cities by improving access from suburbs and handling the movement of people downtown. The old horse-drawn omnibus gave way to horse-drawn streetcars on tracks and then to electric trolleys and elevated railways faster than most people could fathom. In 1890 about 70 percent of urban trolley lines were horse-drawn; by 1900 the figure had dwindled to 2 percent. New lines pushed outward from the city, swallowing nearby villages and converting open land into suburbs. In 1880 about 34 percent of Milwaukee's population lived within a mile of its business center; by 1900 that figure had been cut in half.

Expanding cities required more housing, water, gas, electricity, and waste disposal, to say nothing of better streets to handle heavier flows of traffic. Called upon to provide more services than ever before, city fathers turned to technology for the solution. The condition of streets in American cities was notorious. Most cities still surfaced streets with cobblestone, though Washington, Buffalo, and Philadelphia adopted the European technique of paving with asphalt in the 1880s while others used bricks. By 1900 most cities had learned how to prepare better foundations and cover their streets with cheap, quiet, durable macadam.

Part of the problem was that streets rarely lay undis-
turbed. Cities were always ripping them up to install pipes,
cables, tubing, or sewers. Despite the rapid spread of sewer
lines, nothing solved the mountainous accumulation of
waste. Most cities dumped their sewage into nearby seas or
rivers; New York alone was choking its rivers with 500
million gallons of raw sewage a day by 1916. Chicago
resorted to the drastic plan of reversing the flow of the
Chicago River away from Lake Michigan so as to carry its
sewage downstream to the Mississippi River. But the $80
million scheme also polluted downstream rivers and towns
with its wastes, and the system backed up into Chicago and
Lake Michigan during heavy rains.

Water systems also struggled to keep up with growing
populations. New York's thirty-four-mile Croton aqueduct
was hailed as a modern wonder when it opened in 1842, but
half a century later the city had to build a second aqueduct
carrying four times the amount as the original. Even that
was not enough, and New York erected a third line a
hundred miles up the Hudson River to tap water from the
Catskills at a cost of $180 million. In the water-starved West
the small city of Los Angeles traveled 250 miles to secure
water from the Sierra Mountains, using enough cement in
its system to build a wall ten feet thick and forty feet high
around Manhattan Island.

It didn't help that most cities drew their drinking water
from the same place where they dumped their garbage and
waste. Long before 1900 pure water had become extinct
around most large cities, forcing them to purify their supply
with tons of chemicals to make it drinkable and prevent
disease. In 1870 no American city had a water filtration
system; thirty years later only 6 percent of the urban
population received filtered water. By 1920, however, most
large cities had installed filtration and treatment plants.

Jersey City led the way with a chemical treatment plant in 1908, while Pittsburgh waited until its death rate from typhoid fever reached four times the national average before building a filter treatment system.

Urban growth fed on technology, which powered cities, expanded them upward and outward, provided their water, light, and heat, carried off their wastes, and organized their work patterns. Much of this got done crudely, inefficiently, and at a human cost few Americans cared to reckon or even consider. It was far easier to view technology as a tool of progress than to see the ways in which that progress was itself a treadmill on which every solution spawned another set of problems. A pattern evolved of welcoming new and improved technology as the solution to every dilemma with little regard for the problems that might arise from its use.

Nowadays we tend to forget that the automobile was hailed as the savior of the city from pollution—in this case horse manure. In 1907 the 12,500 horses in the city of Milwaukee deposited 133 tons of manure on the streets every day. The automobile got rid of those piles but turned out to have some pollutants of its own. Mass transit and bridges were supposed to relieve cities of congestion. Instead they clustered people in dense communities around transportation lines and accelerated the trend of abandoning the inner city to a core inhabited by businesses and the poor.

Every new technology brought problems along with its possibilities. Some were more lethal than others. No one worshiped more reverently at the altar of technology than E. W. Byrn, an official in the Patent Office. Writing in 1900 he lavished praise on a mysterious new discovery called the x-ray which represented "the greatest addition to the surgeon's resources that has ever been made in the form of mechanical appliances." Here was a technology that also qualified as a wonder of nature, though Byrn noted in passing that repeated exposure produced a "peculiar physiological effect...a severe effect on the skin, somewhat resembling sunburn." Not for many years would this effect of radiation be fully understood, by which time many people had suffered serious and often fatal sickness.

Lethal or otherwise, galloping technology had clearly planted itself center stage in American life well before the turn of the century. Nothing illustrates this fact better than the gigantic Centennial Exhibition held in Philadelphia during the summer of 1876. Amid the wonders found in its 249 buildings sprawled over 284 acres of land, nothing attracted more attention or excited more people than Machinery Hall. Housed within its 510,000 square feet of space were examples of every breed of advanced technology: machines for grinding, milling, pressing, punching, sewing, printing, drilling, polishing, hammering, and pumping, along with engines, no less than seventy-five locomotives, and even a small working model oil well.

Every one of the active machines drew its power from the mighty Corliss steam engine, looming forty feet high, weighing seven hundred tons, and churning out 2,500 horsepower. The whole spectacle left visitors awestruck. An elderly Ralph Waldo Emerson, the creature of a different world, walked away "dazzled and dumbfounded." One visitor captured this sense in an article for the *Atlantic Monthly* that July, finding

> ...something at once sublime and infernal in the spectacle. Machines claim nothing for themselves; they make no boasts, but silently perform their task before your eyes; the mode in which it is effected is a mystery; the spools, spindles, shuttles are there, so is the raw material. One sees the means and the result, but the process is invisible and inscrutable as those of Nature.... Nowhere else are the triumphs of ingenuity, marvels of skill, so displayed, so demonstrated.

The popularity of the exhibit, and the enthusiastic responses to it, revealed some important insights into the role of technology in American life. No one could mistake the depth or passion of the American love affair with technology, or the pride most people felt in these machines as a measure— even a boast—of the superiority of American civilization. Nor could they doubt that Americans measured progress in material terms and regarded technology as the primary tool for its advancement.

But one revealing lesson got overlooked entirely. Machinery Hall was a state-of-the-art exhibit, showing the forefront of modern technology. By 1900 or shortly afterward, virtually every machine in the display was deemed quaint if not obsolete. To a crowd wandering through the same exhibits after 1900, it would have seemed more like a museum.

# 8

# Integration and Alienation

The Clock in the workshop,—it rests not a moment;
It points on, and ticks on: eternity—time;
Once someone told me the clock had a meaning,—
In pointing and ticking had reason and rhyme....
At times, when I listen, I hear the clock plainly;—
The reason of old—the old meaning—is gone!
The maddening pendulum urges me forward
To labor and still labor on.
The tick of the clock is the boss in his anger.
The face of the clock has the eyes of the foe.
The clock—I shudder—Dost hear how it draws me?
It calls me "Machine" and it cries me "Sew"!
—Morris Rosenfeld,
*Songs of Labor and Other Poems* (1914)

THE RISE OF the industrial economy was an unbroken march, but not always a triumphal one. Like most human activity, it matched gains in some areas with setbacks in others. Many of the latter were what came to be known as social overhead costs, which were not as obvious or spectacular as the surge in productivity. They ranged from physical blights such as environmental damage and health hazards, to social disorders like slums and rising crime rates, to psychological tolls exacted by stress, poverty, constant change, and social dislocation.

A curious paradox marked this pattern of growth: the more integrated the corporate economy became, the more alienated the corporate society grew. The more organized and formal American life became, the more volatile and fragmented it grew. The parts of American society became larger, more numerous, and more intricate than ever before, but they didn't add up to any clear or meaningful whole. Indeed, critics insisted that some parts threatened others and didn't belong there at all. The obvious, often boisterous pride people took in being Americans was exceeded only by their confusion and disagreement over what being American meant. Not only did it mean different things to different people, there were many more different kinds of people to whom it meant different things.

David Potter explained this paradox as an outcome of the influence of abundance on American life. "American conditions," he wrote, "...brought about a condition of mobility far more widespread and pervasive than any previous society or previous era of history had ever witnessed." At the same time, "the economic potentialities of our continent have caused us to subordinate other values to the realization of maximum wealth." The stress on economic growth led Americans to downplay or ignore other aspects of social development, just as the emphasis on maximizing individual freedom to promote this growth led us to define equality not as a level of status but as a level playing field:

> Equality came to mean...parity in competition. Its value was as a means to advancement rather than as an asset in itself....Democracy made this promise, but the riches of North America fulfilled it; and our democratic system... survived because an economic surplus was available to pay democracy's promissory notes....Our system of equality removes certain negative impediments to success, and

then our positive access to a larger measure of abundance permits fulfillment of the success promise.... It is a fact which we have consistently and effectively suppressed in the national consciousness.

In this open system, maximizing individual freedom gave the most talented entrepreneurs free rein to create what became giant enterprises that closed out the playing field in that industry to newcomers. It also allowed a growing array of social problems to accumulate and worsen because responsibility for social policy was divided and lacking in clout or vision. The myth of the American Dream was a magnet that drew immigrants to these shores in search of a new life. These newcomers were welcomed for the cheap labor they provided but despised for the strange customs and values they brought.

This clash between economic opportunity and social harmony had been present from the beginning. A much earlier generation of Americans had introduced slavery into the nation with little concern for its broader effects on society in the long run. Individual planters viewed it as a reliable source of much-needed labor, slave traders as a source of profit; they were not responsible for the larger society. From their actions flowed more than two centuries of racial strife as well as a bloody civil war that nearly brought down the nation. So too with the treatment of Native Americans, who were viewed as obstacles to economic development above any other consideration, or the environment, whose resources were considered fair game for individuals seeking their fortunes, regardless of long-term damage.

In these and many other cases, individuals achieved impressive, often spectacular short-term personal gains for which the larger society paid dearly in the longer run. It was not that the people who profited were greedy, shortsighted villains (though some surely were) but rather that the nation's value system, shaped by abundance, encouraged this pattern of development. This was, after all, what the magical phrase "America, the Land of Opportunity" meant to most people. Opportunity was above all else an open door, not a guide to social responsibility.

The 1880s emerged as the key decade for the integration of the corporate economy. While only a few industries reached the stage of integrating both production and distribution within their operation, others soon followed. A growing population, galloping technology, and new organizational vision forged within a remarkably short time a national market for products from corporations that in many cases had begun to serve not only national but global markets as well.

During the 1880s the railroad and telegraph industries marched steadily toward consolidation and integration, thereby accelerating the flow of goods and information. Railroads moved to a standard gauge, standard time, and more standardized equipment to expedite shipment across the lines of different companies. Mergers gradually reduced a large number of roads into a handful of giant systems, though no single company ever managed to span the entire continent. Western Union continued to absorb rival telegraph companies and to expand facilities. The 9,077 offices it operated in 1880 doubled to 18,470 by the decade's end.

Railroad and telegraph companies alike grew to mammoth sizes by performing one basic function. Some emerging corporate giants of the 1880s carried growth to another level by integrating several complex functions. They did this out of necessity, driven by two types of problems. One group of companies so improved their output through new technology that they could produce far more than existing markets could buy. The other group manufactured products specialized enough to require marketing support services. Both made the bold decision to provide what they needed within their own operation, and moved to integrate production with purchasing and distribution.

Examples of the first group include manufacturers of cigarettes, breakfast cereal, canned soup and fruit, flour, and matches, whose production took quantum leaps thanks to new machines. To sell their huge output they resorted to mass advertising of brand names, thereby transforming an old technique into a new industry. Once James B. Duke could produce 240,000 cigarettes a day, he advertised lavishly, built a vast sales organization at home and abroad, and created an elaborate purchasing network to assure his tobacco supply. By 1889 he was producing 834 million cigarettes with sales of $4.5 million a year; he was also spending $800,000 annually on advertising. The next year Duke brought four competitors into a new colossus, the American Tobacco Company.

Manufacturers of perishable products followed the same path. Here the pioneer was Gustavus Swift, the first meat packer to grasp the importance of a distribution network. When Swift arrived in Chicago in 1875, almost all meat still moved east as cattle to be slaughtered by local butchers. Swift built up a vast slaughtering operation in Chicago and supplemented it with a network of branch houses throughout the country to store, sell, and deliver meat moved there by refrigerator car. Local butchers fought him bitterly, trying to inflame consumer fears over meat produced days or weeks earlier hundreds of miles away. But Swift routed them by offering quality products at low prices.

Swift's success forced other packers to follow suit until the meat industry became dominated by a handful of firms selling and advertising nationally. Brewers went the same route during the 1880s after a new malting process provided better speed and improved control in brewing. Augustus Busch, Joseph Pabst, and Joseph Schlitz emerged as leaders of the industry by transforming local breweries into national operations that did their own marketing and relied heavily on advertising to win business from local beers.

A second group of products, more costly and complex, could not be sold in quantity without the assurance of support services such as demonstrations, credit, and repair service. These included sewing machines, office machines, agricultural equipment, elevators, pumps, and printing presses. Singer Sewing Machine Company evolved into an integrated operation with its own network of marketing and distribution offices on a global scale along with its own factories for producing the machines. By the 1890s it also owned foundries, timberlands, and some of its own transportation facilities.

Farm machinery firms followed the McCormick Company in pursuing this same pattern, while John H. Patterson's National Cash Register led the parade of office machine companies toward integrated operations. Electrical equipment manufacturers fell in line, as did such firms as A. B. Dick, Burroughs, Otis Elevator, and two American staples, Wrigley chewing gum and Coca-Cola. Some companies simply grew larger through horizontal integration—that is, by merging with other firms that performed the same function or made the same product. This type of merger rarely proved enduring unless the new company also integrated vertically by reaching back toward sources of raw materials and/or forward toward distribution and marketing. Standard Oil was the most spectacular example of a company moving successfully from horizontal to vertical integration.

Banking underwent this same transformation. Indeed, its

growth as an industry tracked the rise of large railroad and industrial corporations. In 1870 the nation had 1,937 banks with assets of nearly $1.8 billion; these figures soared to 13,053 banks with nearly $11.4 billion in assets by 1900 and 30,909 banks with more than $53 billion in assets by 1920. Most banks, like most businesses, remained small and local; the major ones consolidated and integrated their functions much like manufacturing firms. New York emerged as the nation's financial center and the home of its largest, most powerful banks.

Two types of institutions dominated the banking scene. *Commercial* banks performed the whole range of banking services for the public. *Investment* banking firms emerged during the nineteenth century as specialists in handling and marketing issues of securities for corporations. As Vincent P. Carosso described it, the investment banker's job was "to serve the users and suppliers of capital by providing the facilities through which savings are channeled into long-term investment." Investment bankers did not deal with the general public and performed other banking services only for their select clients. The best-known banker in the United States, J. P. Morgan, epitomized the breed.

As the industrial economy expanded, the role of investment bankers grew more important. Railroads, as the nation's first big business, became their first major clients and remained so until late in the century. When railroads needed capital to build lines or buy equipment, they issued stocks or bonds which the bankers then sold to the general public. Mergers and reorganizations also required large amounts of capital, which the bankers supplied. Gradually the bankers took seats on the boards of their client railroads and influenced management policies. The extent of their business can be illustrated by the fact that between 1885 and 1900 bond issues alone totaled more than $6.4 billion.

Late in the century industrial firms began to supplant railroads as the core of investment banker business. Growing firms incorporated or merged with other companies, needed capital for expansion or new machinery, and so decided to make public offerings of their securities. "It is astonishing the amount of working capital you must have in a great concern," remarked Andrew Carnegie. "It is far more than the cost of the works." New Jersey's liberal incorporation law of 1889, the Sherman Antitrust Act of 1890, and other factors spurred an epidemic of mergers among American firms between 1895 and 1904. These developments all fed business to investment bankers, increasing not only their wealth but their influence as well.

The larger commercial banks could not help but notice this lucrative market. Some, like the First National Bank of New York, had always done investment banking; others began moving into the field and grew to enormous size. The best known and most powerful of these was the National City Bank of New York. Under the astute leadership of James Stillman and Frank Vanderlip, National City diversified its activities and integrated its organization. Other banks did the same, and during the 1900s the industry marched toward what Fritz Redlich called "department-store banking" in the 1920s.

As the larger banks consolidated their organizations, integrated their functions, and diversified their activities, they exerted a growing power over the business world. "Big deals are not possible if banking assistance is withheld," observed an industry journal in 1899. The competition for business sometimes drew the great bankers together in alliances. Stillman, for example, grew close to Jacob H. Schiff, the senior partner of Kuhn, Loeb, an investment banking firm second only to Morgan's. A third associate lent even more clout to this connection: William Rockefeller, brother of John and a powerful business figure in his own right. This trio of associates then allied themselves to the most talented and dynamic railroad man of the era, himself a banker by trade, E. H. Harriman.

The bankers grew powerful not only because of the vital role they played in an industrial system that was growing and integrating, but also because the nation's prosperity provided huge sums of money seeking investments such as new securities. One major source of capital seeking investment was insurance companies, whose resources vaulted from $403 million in 1875 to $1.7 billion in 1900. The giant insurance companies poured huge sums into railroad bonds and other securities. Not surprisingly, the heads of these firms drew close to the bankers who handled their investments.

This pattern of integration alarmed the public because it was accompanied by an interlocking of the men who sat astride these huge new combinations. To an earlier generation the villain of the movement had been John D. Rockefeller and his Standard Oil Trust. By 1910, however, critics railed at what they called the "Money Trust" as the greater threat. Louis D. Brandeis, who grew rich as a corporation lawyer before carving out a distinguished career on the Supreme Court, startled Americans in 1913 with a little book entitled *Other People's Money*, in which he said:

> The dominant element in our financial hierarchy is the investment banker. Associated banks, trust companies and life insurance companies are his tools. Controlled railroads, public service and industrial corporations are his subjects. Though properly but middlemen, these bankers bestride as masters America's business world, so that practically no larger enterprise can be undertaken successfully without their participation and approval.... The key to their power is combination—concentration intensive and comprehensive.

The quiet, velvety Stillman put it more succinctly. When young Henry Morgenthau marveled at the profit from one transaction, Stillman silenced him by saying, "Morgenthau, you don't understand what profits we are in the habit of making."

The outcry against profits that seemed obscene made by men who wielded enormous power was but one symptom of the growing alienation throughout the corporate society. What made it distinctive was the way in which it revealed the direct connection between two elemental forces: here was a concrete example of integration producing alienation.

The political upheavals that took place between 1900 and 1917 have long been known as the Progressive movement, even though historians have yet to figure out exactly what that movement was or whether it was actually a movement at all. Most of its reform efforts targeted abuses or problems that were by-products of industrialization, such as slums, child labor, and urban political corruption. One common theme haunted much of the activity labeled "progressive" during these years: a fear of bigness, especially the looming power of giant corporations but also less tangible forms like the sprawling strangeness of growing cities, the well-oiled political machines, and the invisible web of moneyed interests who seemed to have their hands in every pie that mattered.

In broader terms this fear of bigness was a revolt against modernism, a protest against the forces that were ripping apart the familiar fabric of American life. The corporate society was, in Thomas Kuhn's overused but still useful concept, a new paradigm, and like all true paradigms it was incompatible with the preceding one. Not all believers in progressive causes shared this fear, but a surprising number embodied this theme. This was hardly surprising. As a new paradigm the corporate society brought deep and bitter divisions to American life, opening new conflicts and aggravating old ones. Most of these conflicts could be seen with painful clarity in the fast-growing industrial cities that were both the shame and the showcases of the corporate society.

Newcomers to the industrial city could not have felt less at home if they had arrived on another planet. The small town of the new world or village of the old world was a place of friends and familiar faces. The city was a place of strangers and strangeness, always in motion. It was an alien place with its own landscape, rhythms, languages and customs, foods, entertainments, spectacles, and, above all, a towering indifference toward those looking to it for the smallest shred of something familiar. It was the great seething marketplace of the corporate economy, the arena in which business rivals clashed for stakes large and small, and strange cultures rubbed uneasily against one another in tectonic neighborhoods.

The industrial city was not only alien and intimidating but appalling as well. Rural America had its foul sights and smells as well, but never piled together in so great a quantity in so tight an area. Aside from monuments and other objects of beauty, industrial cities housed the foulest environment yet known to man. Coal-burning smokestacks blackened lungs as well as buildings. Streets reeked with animal waste, garbage, and overflowing septic systems that sometimes made them all but impassable.

Different industries gave each city its own special flavor. Early New York City had the "Swamp," a district where tanners cooked their vile-smelling vats of brew. A perpetual gloom of smoke from the iron and steel mills enveloped Pittsburgh and other cities. The distinguished English sociologist Herbert Spencer took one look at Pittsburgh and shocked his hosts by declaring that "Six months' residence here would justify suicide." A disgusted Cincinnati editor described in 1874 "an atmosphere heavy with the odors of death and decay and animal filth and steaming nastiness of every description" created by "mammoth slaughter-houses, enormous rendering establishments, vast soap and candle factories, immense hog-pens and gigantic tanneries." H. L. Mencken recalled a Baltimore that smelled "like a billion polecats."

For everyone, especially the poor, this mix of stench and slop brought sickness as well as disgust: epidemics of typhoid fever in the summer and malaria in the autumn, periodic outbreaks of diphtheria, smallpox, or cholera, and constant plagues of dysentery and tuberculosis—the "White Death" that killed more Americans than any other disease during this era. One tenement district in New York was dubbed the "lung block" because so many of its residents suffered from tuberculosis. Late in the century many of these diseases were brought under control thanks to dramatic advances in understanding germ theory, but relief came slowly to the poor who lived in overcrowded tenements with little clean water, fresh air, or decent sanitation.

Chicago observers cringed at the sight of three hundred children working in the stockyards, "scores of them standing ankle-deep in blood and refuse, as they do the work of butchers." Not far from the White House in Washington lay a black slum called "Murder Bay," where health officials watched poor black families scrounge their dinners from garbage cans and dumps. In every city the poor paid high rents for old and inadequate housing by jamming as many people as possible into every room. One thirty-two-acre section of New York owned the dubious honor of being the most congested neighborhood in the world. It housed thirty thousand people in a six-block area, about 986 people per acre compared with 485 people in Prague, which had the worst slum in Europe, or 760 in Bombay, site of the most crowded slum found anywhere else in the world.

Through these noisy, teeming neighborhoods in every industrial city stalked everything the "better class" of people feared most: crime, poverty, disease, the human fuel of corrupt political machines, and things foreign. The fact that these were all ethnic or racial neighborhoods made it easy for other people to associate their evils, real or imagined, with the "foreignness" of the inhabitants. They had strange customs, practiced strange religions, dressed in odd clothes, ate weird foods, and spoke incomprehensible languages. A small town or country village might have a few such people along with some black folk, but industrial cities had thousands of them with more coming all the time. Jacob Riis calculated that in 1890 New York had "half as many Italians as Naples, as many Germans as Hamburg, twice as many Irish as Dublin, and two and a half times the number of Jews in Warsaw." Jane Addams described the neighborhood surrounding Hull House in Chicago this way:

> Between Halsted Street and the river live about ten thousand Italians: Neapolitans, Sicilians, and Calabrians, with an occasional Lombard or Venetian. To the South on Twelfth Street are many Germans, and side streets are given over almost entirely to Polish and Russian Jews. Further south, three Jewish colonies merge into a huge Bohemian colony, so vast that Chicago ranks as the third Bohemian city in the world. To the north-west are many Canadians—French, clannish in spite of their long residence in America, and to the north are many Irish and first-generation Americans.

The "better class" shook their heads in dismay at spectacles like this; clearly these intruders were "not one of us" and posed a threat to "our way of life." But who was us?

The "better class" considered themselves native Americans—
long before that term acquired an altogether different meaning—and the keepers of American cultural traditions. As a
nation of immigrants the United States did not have long
traditions, and certainly no one tradition that might be
called *the* American way of life. From colonial times differences in customs and values ran deep within American
society and often erupted into violence or upheaval. The
Civil War is only the most obvious and bloody example of
this cultural conflict.

But one cluster of values came to dominate American
culture in all regions. It consisted of those attitudes, beliefs,
and customs known popularly as White Anglo-Saxon Protestant (WASP) culture. The families who ruled America,
who stood at the top of the economic and social ladders,
mostly belonged to this group, whose members tended to
keep its ranks closed by marrying among themselves. Many
if not most Americans did not qualify for membership in
this nebulous congregation, and its own self-appointed
spokesmen did not always agree on what they were defend-
ing from whom. But the belief circulated widely that a
distinctive American way of life existed and must be preserved from foreign influence.

Earlier this obsession with racial purity and cultural
integrity had revealed itself in violent opposition to the Irish,
the Catholic church, freemasonry, radicalism, and above all
in the clash over slavery. A deep strain of racial prejudice
ran through American society; even many of those who
fervently opposed slavery could not conceive that black
Americans could ever mix with whites on equal terms.
Racism was a way of life in the United States, embedded in
its culture as well as its social theory. Similar attitudes
extended to foreign immigrants, especially when the flow of
newcomers shifted from the familiar ethnic mixes of north-

western Europe to the rainbow of peoples from southern and eastern Europe.

Historian Robert Wiebe described the United States in the 1870s as a society of "island communities," lacking a core of central authority or institutions that might have imposed some order on the changes wrought by industrialization. "American institutions," he added, "were still oriented toward a community life where family and church, education and press, professions and government, all largely found their meanings by the way they fit one with another inside a town or a detached portion of a city."

These island communities were mostly dominated by local elites whose families had been there for generations and often helped found the town. They embraced the gospel of WASP culture as the American way and were accustomed to presiding over a community of familiar faces where people knew their place. The spectacular growth fueled by industrialism disrupted this old order by making the nation's population far more multicultural than it had ever been, and by swelling the populations of cities and towns to the point where the old ruling elite could no longer exert its usual control.

No ruling class surrenders power and status easily, even in a democracy. Nativists found it easy to blame "foreigners" for most of the dislocation and social tensions wrought by industrialization. The old rural suspicion of urban America reached new heights of fear and loathing as cities grew like mushrooms, filled up with foreigners, and boiled over with problems that led one reformer to label them "civilization's inferno." In 1885 a Congregationalist minister from the Midwest, Josiah Strong, distilled these fears into an immensely popular book called *Our Country*.

Imbued with Strong's unshakable belief in the cultural superiority of white Anglo-Saxon Protestant values, the book itemized the threats posed to American civilization and its way of life. The typical immigrant, he said, "not only furnishes the greater portion of our criminals" but "is also seriously affecting the morals of the native population." From this ominous base of immigrants accumulating in the cities, Strong traced out a pattern of evils: crime, intemperance, Romanism (Catholicism), political corruption, socialism, and the modern city itself:

> The city has become a serious menace to our civilization because in it...each of the dangers we have discussed is enhanced, and all are focalized. It has a peculiar attraction for the immigrant....Because our cities are so largely foreign, Romanism finds in them its chief strength. For the same reason the saloon, together with the intemperance and the liquor power which it represents, is multiplied in the city....Here is heaped the social dynamite; here roughs, gamblers, thieves, robbers, lawless and desperate men of all sorts, congregate...here gather foreigners and wage-workers who are especially susceptible to socialist arguments.

Strong intertwined these themes of fear in masterful fashion, but he was far from the first to do it. In 1872 Charles Loring Brace had warned against the presence of large numbers of impoverished immigrants in New York:

> Thousands are children of poor foreigners, who have permitted them to grow up without school, education, or religion. All the neglect and bad education and evil example of a poor class tend to...swell the ranks of ruffians and criminals. So, at length, a great multitude of ignorant, untrained, passionate, irreligious boys and young men...become the "dangerous" class of the city.

A New York judge minced no words when he declared that "there is a large class—I was about to say a majority—of the population of New York and Brooklyn...to whom the rearing of two or more children means inevitably a boy for the penitentiary, and a girl for the brothel."

This flood of nativist reaction reached its peak in 1916 with the appearance of *The Passing of the Great Race* by conservative lawyer Madison Grant. Pretending to scientific detachment on the subject, Grant warned that the deluge of new immigrants contained

> a large and increasing number of the weak, the broken and the mentally crippled of all races drawn from the lowest stratum of the Mediterranean basin and the Balkans, together with the hordes of the wretched, submerged populations of the Polish ghettoes. Our jails, insane asylums and almshouses are filled with this human flotsam and the whole tone of American life, social, moral and political, has been lowered and vulgarized by them.

Predictably, organizations sprang up to combat these threats. The American Protective Association (1876) led the antiimmigrant crusade, followed by the Immigration Restriction League and smaller groups. These organizations launched a political movement to limit immigration. Presidents Grover Cleveland (1896) and William Howard Taft (1913) vetoed bills that would have required a literacy test, but the restriction campaign finally tasted victory in 1921 with the passage of an act establishing the first quota system on immigration. The act limited immigration in any year to 3 percent of the number of each nationality already in the United States; a second act in 1924 halved this figure and permanently closed the gate for massive immigration.

Nativists saw in the great wave of immigration not a reflection of currents that had swept through American life since the first settlers arrived, but rather a tidal surge that threatened their culture in two distinct ways. On one level it undermined the supremacy of WASP values that infused American society in hundreds of ways, often subtle and indirect. More directly it threatened their political control of society, especially at the local level where the weight of popular votes was felt more immediately.

These fears were confirmed when city after city ousted the old ruling elite in favor of political machines rooted solidly in the ethnic neighborhoods. This displaced elite regarded its downfall not merely as a loss of power but as a menace to the process of democracy that was the cornerstone of the American way. It never occurred to them that the political machines, which they denounced as corrupt and decadent, were in fact (as their name implied) efficient organizations created to fill an enormous vacuum in American society caused by the inability of urban government to cope with the strains of rapid growth.

Lincoln Steffens was among the few who saw what was happening. When reformers dethroned the bosses and gained office, they meant well but did not know how to run the city as a business. They showed little interest in the poor, tried to impose economy and eliminate corruption, and ended up snarling City Hall in red tape until annoyed voters threw them out. "The clergy had governed Boston once," observed Steffens sagely, "then the aristocracy, then the leading businessmen. All these forms of goodness had had their day. Let's give up the good men and try the strong men."

The problem with many if not most of the reformers who cried for efficiency, honesty, and good government was that they were apostles of the WASP creed of values and therefore indifferent if not hostile to the broader social problems of the cities. Their class and ethnic prejudices blinded them to the actual functions performed by the machine. Brand Whitlock, a reform mayor of Toledo, was an exception to this rule. "The word 'reformer' like the word 'politician' had degenerated," he mused in 1914, "and in the mind of the common man, come to connote something very disagreeable. In four terms as mayor I came to know both species pretty well, and... I prefer politician. He, at least, is human."

The social problems spawned by immigration presented reformers with an even greater dilemma. Beyond the immediate issues of jobs, housing, and education lay the thorny issue of what to do about clashing cultures. If, as nativists and reformers alike insisted, the newcomers had no sense of American institutions, the obvious solution was to "Americanize" them. This approach meant stripping them of their former identities and integrating them into American society as full-fledged citizens.

Apart from the pain and suffering inflicted on the newcomers, this approach presented nativists with an awkward dilemma. Most wanted to assimilate the immigrants but not integrate them, wished to "Americanize" them but did not want them moving into their neighborhoods, joining their clubs, marrying their daughters, or even attending their schools. This same dilemma had arisen after the Civil War, when most Americans applauded the end of slavery but fiercely opposed efforts to make black Americans full-fledged citizens and violently resisted attempts to integrate them into society as equals. Asians, Hispanics, and Native Americans experienced similar hostility in different parts of the nation.

The assimilation dilemma emerged early as the major problem of American society and has remained so ever since. What has changed over time is the ethnic or racial background of the newcomers; the debate has changed little beyond toning down its more overt racist rhetoric. The central dilemma of American history has been how to create a unified nation out of so many diverse cultural traditions and values. More often than not the effort has alienated more than it integrated, and the balance between pluralism and assimilation remains a delicate one. The battle over assimilation began with the first waves of Irish immigrants in the 1840s and took on fresh urgency during the great immigration of 1880–1914, when the United States became a truly multicultural nation.

Education became a logical battleground for this fight. The public school movement, which had just gained widespread acceptance by the time of the Civil War, had always linked progress with education. In the industrial cities, with their surging populations, public schools faced a new challenge: not merely to educate but to Americanize as well. To Professor Ellwood P. Cubberley of Stanford and many others, this meant purging the immigrants of their ethnic heritage and replacing it with WASP values. The first task of education, proclaimed Cubberley, was to "assimilate and amalgamate these people as a part of our American race, and to implant in their children...the Anglo-Saxon conception of righteousness, law and order, and popular government."

A member of the Daughters of the American Revolution put the matter far more succinctly when she asked, "What can you expect of the Americanism of the man whose breath always reeks of garlic?"

Advocates of this view argued that Americanization meant teaching newcomers the core values of what historian Lawrence Cremin described as "the true, historic America, the America worth preserving." Not surprisingly, most of those who espoused this belief were white Anglo-Saxon Protestants. Others countered that any form of national unity had to be grounded in a new breed of nationality that was beginning to emerge, one based on cultural pluralism. Some defenders of the WASP core culture blithely underestimated the problem facing them. "We used to have an Americanization problem," boasted one, "but we haven't got one any longer. Several years ago we got all the foreigners in our town in some English and civics classes and in two or three months we Americanized 'em all."

Few cities could come close to getting all the newcomers into classes. A 1909 study by the United States Immigration Commission showed that almost 58 percent of the children in the schools of thirty-seven major cities had foreign-born parents. In such diverse cities as Chelsea, Massachusetts, and Duluth, Minnesota, the figure exceeded 74 percent; New York had nearly 72 percent, Chicago 67 percent, and Boston 64 percent. The schools themselves groaned from overcrowding and classes so large they seldom rose above chaos. "For one person to teach 150 children is an impossible task," conceded an 1895 survey of a Brooklyn public school. "...If a parent were offered the alternative of having his child go to school in a cellar, or of sharing in the one hundred and fiftieth part of the time of a tired, overworked teacher, he might well hesitate before he decided."

Still, people clung to the belief that, as a New York high school principal put it, "Education will solve every problem of our national life, even that of assimilating our foreign element." But some resisted assimilation on the terms offered. The Catholic church set the tone early by going so far as to erect its own parallel school system to serve immigrant Catholics who objected to the prejudice against their religion so common in the public schools. Thoughtful reformers like Jane Addams recognized that assimilation was a two-edged sword and understood the toll it exacted from newcomers:

> And yet in spite of the fact that the public school is the great savior of the immigrant district, and the one agency which inducts the children into the changed conditions of

American life,...the school too often separates the child from his parents and widens the old gulf between fathers and sons which is never so cruel and so wide as it is between the immigrants who came to this country and their children who have gone to the public school and feel that they have learned it all.

Throughout this period assimilation remained the most noble of ideals and most imperfect of processes. Less was said about those who were simply rejected by society on racial grounds. Their alienation was far more cruel and lasting. Black Americans had been in the country far longer than most white people but had always been regarded as alien and inferior. In 1900 they were barely a generation past slavery, and the blessings of freedom had done little to elevate their status. Segregation by law and custom ruled almost everywhere, denying blacks even such basic privileges as the right to vote or that most cherished of American ideals, equality of opportunity.

Before the Civil War the black population had been confined largely to the South, where it was scattered about the rural landscape. During the industrial era blacks migrated steadily to cities north and south, where they piled up in ghettos far more rigid in their separation than the ethnic ghettos. The doorways of advancement open to ambitious immigrants stayed tightly shut to blacks. No group endured more systematic exclusion from jobs, social advancement, and schools. For them the ghetto became not a way station on the road to a better life but a permanent residence. Where ethnic ghettos gradually broke up, the black ghetto became a way of life and ultimately its own culture outside the mainstream of white society.

Asians encountered similar restrictions for the same reason. Of all the differences that separated minorities from the mainstream of American life, none loomed so large as color. Asians got the worst of both worlds: they were foreign immigrants whose race doomed them to the same treatment afforded blacks and Native Americans. They too clustered in tight neighborhoods and endured sporadic outbreaks of hostility and violence along with systematic discrimination. In 1882 the Chinese Exclusion Act became the first of a series of restrictive acts that shut down virtually all Asian immigration by 1924.

The alienation of these groups could not have been more complete because they saw no way out, no future that promised anything better for their children. Later generations liked to capture this experience with the metaphor of the melting pot, but a more apt image would have been the salad bowl, in which all the different ingredients were mixed together but never quite blended. Thanks in large measure to this bitter paradox of integration and alienation, American society remained one in which the parts never quite added up to a whole.

# 9

# The Flowering of the Third America

Modern civilization, in becoming more complex and
refined, has become more exacting. It discerns more
benefits which the organized power of government
can secure, and grows more anxious to attain them.
Men live fast, and are impatient of the slow working
of natural laws.

—Lord James Bryce,
*The American Commonwealth* (1888)

THERE HAVE BEEN five Americas in our history, each
one defined by economic forces that swept away one society
and ushered in another. The first embraced the colonial
period, when ties with England dominated economic life.
The second, extending from the Revolution to the Civil War,
featured an agrarian economy in which slavery played a
prominent part. The third embraced the industrial transformation between 1865 and 1920. The fourth emerged after
World War I, shaped by the forces discussed in this chapter
and described briefly in the epilogue. The fifth arose after
World War II and is already giving way to a sixth.

None of these eras inflicted more confusion or caused
more dislocation than the third one. Converting a rural,
agrarian society to an urban, industrial one changed the lives
of people in more basic ways than in any other period. Later
eras may have introduced change more rapidly, but their

*degree* of change cannot compare with this first entrance into the industrial age. Since 1920 Americans have grown much more accustomed to change as a constant in their lives.

By the eve of World War I the third America had come of age and was reshaping the course of national life in new directions. The corporate economy led the way by continuing its relentless march toward integration and improved organization. The pattern of this journey is laid out with remarkable clarity in the 1901 annual report of the National Biscuit Company, a giant created by the merger of three smaller firms:

> This Company is four years old.... When the company started, it was an aggregation of plants. It is now an organized business. When we look back through the four years, we find that a radical change has been wrought into our business. In the past, the managers of large industrial corporations have thought it necessary, for success, to control or limit competition. So, when this company started, it was believed that we must control competition, and that to do this we must either fight competition or buy it. The first meant a ruinous war of prices and great loss of profits; the second, constantly increasing capitalization. Experience soon proved to us that... either of these courses, if persevered in, must bring disaster. This led us to reflect whether it was necessary to control competition.... We soon satisfied ourselves that within the company itself we must look for success.
>
> We turned our attention... to improving the internal management of our own business, to getting the full benefit from purchasing our raw materials in large quantities, to economizing the expense of manufacture, to systematizing and rendering more effective our selling department, and above all... to improving the quality of our goods and the condition in which they should reach the consumer.

This statement summarizes the course followed by many large corporations that shifted from horizontal to vertical integration, and from single- to multifunction organizations. By the eve of World War I, as Alfred Chandler has emphasized, the "modern multiunit industrial enterprise" had become "a standard instrument for managing the production and distribution of goods in America." Of the 278 industrial companies with assets of $20 million or more producing goods in 1917, 236 turned raw or semifinished materials into finished products, 30 were in mining, 7 produced crude oil, and 5 handled agricultural products.

Those firms did best and grew fastest that relied on large capital investment and heavy use of machinery and energy to produce large quantities of goods in a continuous process for mass markets. Companies that depended on hand labor with little use of machinery or energy grew more slowly, if at all, because they could not integrate their functions or create a smooth-flowing, efficient production process. The merger mania described earlier took on a new twist as more companies increased their size and integration through mergers or acquisitions rather than internal growth.

Many firms like the National Biscuit Company reached this status through vertical integration. Mergers of companies performing the same function seldom offered comparable gains in efficiency and productivity as those which brought together complementary functions. An impressive number of large corporations expanded their operations overseas, creating integrated foreign subsidiaries that signaled the rise of what became known as the multinational enterprise.

One product, driven by the genius of one man, defied the conventional pattern and zoomed to the forefront of American industry. Since its inception in the 1880s, the automobile had been considered a plaything of the rich, too expensive and complicated a possession for ordinary citizens. Henry Ford shattered this notion by transforming it from a luxury to a necessity. In the process he pioneered a technology that was to reshape the contours of American life in the twentieth century much as the railroad had done in the nineteenth.

The idea seemed absurd. Most Americans earned less than $500 a year in 1900, and as late as 1903 the total number of cars sold in the United States was a mere 11,235. There was no road network, no support system of gas stations, garages, or other facilities, no dealer network, and no proven method of producing automobiles at high volume and low cost. But Ford, a Michigan machinist and tinkerer turned engineer, had a compelling vision:

> I will build a motor car for the great multitude, constructed of the best materials, by the best men to be hired, after the simplest designs that modern engineering can devise...so low in price that no man making a good salary will be unable to own one—and enjoy with his family the blessing of hours of pleasure in God's great open spaces.

To everyone's astonishment, Ford did exactly that. He founded Ford Motor Company in 1903 and labored through five years and eight prototype models to find the car he wanted. "The way to make automobiles," he insisted, "is... to make them all alike, to make them come from the factory just alike—just like one pin is like another pin when it comes from a pin factory, or one match is like another match when it comes from a match factory." In October 1908 he finally produced his ideal pin: the Model T. It was the most famous car ever created, and possibly the most perfect as a machine.

Built of quality materials such as Vanadium steel, the Model T was tough, simple, durable, light, easy to operate, and cheap. It had only four constructional units: the power plant, frame, front axle, and rear axle, all of which could be easily repaired or replaced. The first version cost $850, but by 1916 Ford had reduced the price to $360; that year he sold 577,036 cars. He devised the first practical moving assembly line for his plant at Highland Park, Michigan, on which the time required to put together a single chassis dropped from 12 hours 28 minutes to 1 hour 33 minutes.

Ford demonstrated that automobiles could be made in large quantities at low cost and thereby gave America what soon became one of the new "necessities" of the consumer economy. The rapid spread of automobiles brought in its wake a whole infrastructure of support and satellite businesses which bored deeply into the everyday habits of both rural and urban America. Ford himself became a national folk hero. He made a quality product, paid the highest wages in the industry, and for his efforts became the country's second billionaire behind John D. Rockefeller.

Although the large industrial corporation dominated the American economy by World War I, not every sector achieved the same remarkable growth and integration. Alfred Chandler offers this persuasive explanation for the factors that were crucial to ultimate success:

> Markets and technology...had a far greater influence in determining size and concentration in American industry than did the quality of entrepreneurship, the availability of capital, or public policy. Entrepreneurial ability can hardly account for the clustering of giant enterprises in some industries and not in others.... An entrepreneur might enlarge or combine existing enterprises, but he rarely built a new one. Such an opportunity came again only with changes in technology and major shifts in markets.

These new giant enterprises, operating on a global scale,

became the largest and most powerful private institutions in the world. Their presence gave the corporate economy a structure that has endured for most of this century. It also provoked outcries of alarm against the power wielded by the men who controlled these firms and the threat they posed to traditional American institutions.

The revolt against bigness took many forms. Predictably, people tried to personify the evils they saw gathering around them. The men who had been so conspicuous in erecting the vast enterprises now drew mixed reviews for the manner in which they had acted out the American Dream. Some hailed the great entrepreneurs as industrial statesmen; others denounced them as "robber barons." Their lavish, extravagant lifestyles were alternately envied and attacked for their excesses. A number of sensational public inquiries fueled the growing resentment against the men who dominated the corporate economy. The Armstrong investigation of 1905 exposed abuses within the life insurance industry, while the Pujo Committee hearings of 1912–1913 laid bare similar problems in the banking industry. Both revealed the complex interlocking of interests among the elite circle of men who ruled the corporate economy.

What bothered people most in these revelations was the enormous power wielded by a small group of men, and the size of the organizations controlled by them. These fears had been impressed on the public consciousness first by the influence of large railroads on state legislatures and then by the first industrial bogeyman, Standard Oil. The sudden proliferation of large firms or "trusts," spurred by the merger mania at the turn of the century, reinforced the belief that giant corporations were seizing control of American life and leaving small individual businessmen little room in which to flourish. Political movements arose first at the state and then at the national level to curb the power of large corporations and restore some sense of "balance" to the corporate economy.

On one level this protest was a revolt against modernism itself. On another level, however, it was a recognition that the maximization of individual freedom had created a potent economy at the price of a badly dislocated social system. This awareness that economic gains involved social costs was not new, but it took on a fresh urgency from the sheer scale of the effects wrought, whether they were the slums and social problems of the city, or the Wisconsin landscape stripped by forty years of feeding its forests to the West's insatiable appetite for wood, or the vast stretches of eroded and wasted land exhausted by farmers and miners, or the stench and sterile landscape created by industrial pollution in every corner of the nation.

The revolt against the large interests took many forms. Efforts were made to curb the power of particular industries by creating state and federal agencies to regulate them. The railroads were the first industry to undergo regulation by state commissions and then, with the passage of the Interstate Commerce Act in 1887, by the federal government. The precedent set by the railroads was later extended to other industries such as electric power, telephone, and other forms of transportation and public services. Most of these attempts produced mixed results as the commissions grappled with enormously complex questions that seldom yielded clear lines of policy.

A second approach went beyond particular industries and tried to curb the power of giantism through federal laws aimed at protecting competition by outlawing restraint of trade. The Sherman Antitrust Act (1890) and the Clayton Antitrust Act (1914) became the cornerstones of this effort, which also produced mixed and confusing results. Although several Supreme Court cases, notably Northern Securities

(1904), Standard Oil (1911), American Tobacco (1911), and Union Pacific–Southern Pacific railroads (1912), broke up large combinations, no consistent policy emerged because no consensus existed on many crucial questions: How big was too big? What constituted restraint of trade in a given industry? How should the threat posed by size be measured against the efficiency achieved through bigness?

These efforts reflected a dogged attempt by Americans to find a middle course between two extremes. Unrestrained individual freedom was no longer a viable or acceptable basis for economic development; its very success had rendered it obsolete. The alternative of state ownership or control had never appealed to Americans and was rejected in every industry except the postal service and a few public service utilities. This left some form of shared control between public and private agencies as the only recourse. The question then became one of determining the proper mix of public and private influence in each case—and this proved so difficult that we have spent most of this century groping for suitable answers.

Within the American framework, shared control was a logical, even inevitable approach for resolving such difficult issues. The object was to find some way of preserving the efficiency and productivity of large firms while curbing abuses from the power they wielded, and to keep the business system open for new ideas and innovations from small entrepreneurs. Gradually it became clear that government had to play new roles in this process at both the state and federal levels. Along with being the policeman enforcing the rules, it had also to protect those elements of nature and society that lacked advocates within the corporate society. To do this it had to transfer resources from one sector to another to maintain a sense of balance.

Predictably, these changed roles triggered political controversies that continue to rage in our own time. Some complained that government did not do enough; others countered that government had grown too big and unwieldy, that it was by nature inefficient and corrupt. As government at every level assumed new functions, it did grow larger and developed the same bureaucracies that characterized the multiunit corporations. This growth occurred less from design than from crisis, especially major upheavals such as war and depression.

In both the public and private sectors the expansion of organizations of all types meant a rapid growth in the white-collar middle class. At a time when American life was becoming more mobile, it was also becoming more stratified. While the rich got richer, the poor did not get poorer, but they fell much farther behind everyone else. The middle class, always an amorphous body, stood as a social buffer between these extremes, as eager to move upward as it was fearful of slipping down, resentful if not frightened of the alien newcomers who roamed the city's streets. Never before in the nation's history had every class been better off econom- ically, and never had there been more tension among them.

The forces of alienation, fueled by the increased flow of immigrants, were fast turning the nation into a multicultural society without a clear center beyond the dominant WASP culture. Bloody conflicts between labor and capital, sporadic outbreaks of radical or nativist violence, and sensationalized accounts of urban crime kept society in a state of constant turmoil. In our entire history four presidents have been assassinated in office; three of those slayings took place between 1865 and 1901. Lynching and random violence against blacks became part of the social fabric in the South, just as murder, vice, and political corruption became staples of the urban scene.

Something was needed to provide so diverse a society with

common ground to which all could relate. Those who pushed hard for "Americanizing" the newcomers believed this common ground would be a reverence for democracy and the American way of life. They were only half right. Most of the newcomers held a keen reverence for American traditions, but not so much the political as the economic ones. The one core value to which everyone subscribed was an unshakable belief in the possibility of a better life, with "better" defined nearly always in material terms.

This belief in the American Dream, in the "rags-to-riches" success myth, exerted an almost mystical hold on the working and middle classes. For many immigrants even the squalor of urban slums represented a step up from the poverty and persecution of the Old World, but most of all it offered an opportunity for themselves or especially their children to advance and prosper. The middle class had climbed far enough up the economic and social ladder to see that the system worked, and could dare dream of greater heights. The upper class had arrived and need only cling to its lofty perch, something many of them failed to do.

Here is another example of how perceptive David Potter was in emphasizing abundance as the key to understanding the American character. Many if not most people improved their lot; more important, they continued to believe fervently in the *possibility* of becoming better off if they worked hard at it. Nothing else did more to defuse the discontent that raged through American society during these years. That discontent was itself largely an expression of fear that the system was closing down, shutting people out from the better life they craved. But disgruntlement tended to vanish as soon as hard times turned into prosperity, jobs became plentiful, and the standard of living resumed its upward course.

Radicalism took shallow root in the United States because it had little to offer most people. It was hard for anyone to imagine a system better suited to exploiting the abundance of resources available. Moreover, the individualist ethic placed responsibility for success or failure squarely on the person rather than the system in which he or she operated. When things went wrong, who was there to blame but oneself? There were no monarchs or rulers beyond officials elected by the people's own vote. They could be (and often were) thrown out of office, but that would hardly cure an economy turned sour.

In short, the United States had become a complex, multicultural nation that relied heavily on the performance of its economy for internal peace and tranquility. Then, around 1900, a new element emerged as an integrating force for the corporate society: the consumer economy. What more logical center for a nation blessed with abundance? The consumer economy provided tangible, even joyous evidence that the system was working. It also became the unifying thread for a culture of diversity by standardizing tastes through consumer products, films, magazines, radio, sports, and other cultural meeting points.

For a nation with radically different racial, ethnic, cultural, and religious traditions, the market was the best if not the only place to develop shared tastes, values, and traditions. Business and technological developments described earlier made this possible by increasing the output of goods and providing them access to national markets. Pundits might have predicted a rising standard of living from these advances, but no one could have foreseen the unifying effect it would have on a society that shared few other tangible values beyond democracy and the open system.

Later generations would sneer at Calvin Coolidge's remark that "The business of America is business," but he was more right than they knew. No other nation developed a greater capacity for productivity or used it to drive an economy rooted in consumer goods on so massive a scale. The transformation of America from a homemade to a store-bought society occurred quickly in the cities, slower in the country, but it came everywhere. Not only did new products make daily life easier and more pleasant, they also kept getting better over time. Through this pattern of creating new goods and improving old ones, the consumer economy fostered a perpetual-motion machine of expectations that left people eagerly wanting something more, something better.

Consumer products served another important function in a society that was so diverse, mobile, and fast losing its roots in older, more distinct cultural heritages. People came increasingly to define themselves less by *who* they were than by *what* they were. Status and success came to be measured more by one's job or profession, and by the possessions one owned. Social critics and novelists had a field day poking fun at this tendency, but it was a logical, even necessary development for people who had shed most other traditional sources of self-identity.

Like it or not, the United States had by 1900 grown too large and diverse to rely on the small-town habits and customs that had once formed its core value system. The inhabitants of a small town knew pretty much who they and their neighbors were; the residents of a newly built suburb were all strangers in a strange land, gathered there from different backgrounds and desperately needing fresh threads of connection. The consumer economy provided a common national vocabulary that soon became the standard language of the American people.

The success of this system depended on the ability to sell goods in quantity as well as produce them. Marketing assumed a primary place in the business world—a fact strikingly illustrated by the meteoric rise of a new industry.

"If we seek an institution that was brought into being by abundance, without previous existence in any form," noted David Potter, "... we will find it... in modern American advertising." Less than a $10 million industry in 1865, advertising soared to $95 million a year by 1900 and $500 million a year by 1919. During the 1920s, when the consumer economy came into its own, advertising executives would command the highest salaries in the corporate world.

The department and chain stores, which dealt in high-volume, low-price goods, learned early the value of advertising in local markets. The mail-order success of Sears owed much to its catalog, a masterpiece of early advertising. But advertising could not emerge as a major force until large companies began to produce consumer goods in volume for national markets. These items required a brand name for ready identification, which enabled them to be heavily advertised.

During the 1880s four consumer items pioneered in advertising their brands on a national scale. Three of them were soaps (Sapolio, Pear's, Ivory); the fourth was Royal Baking Powder. Their success prompted others to follow. By 1889 James B. Duke was spending lavishly on advertising his cigarettes. Henry Crowell did the same for Quaker Oats, as did H. J. Heinz, Campbell Soups, and the makers of Pet Milk. National Biscuit Company created the brand name of Uneeda Biscuit and advertised it heavily. "This is a golden age in trademarks," enthused *Printer's Ink* in 1905:

> Everywhere... there are opportunities to take the lead in advertising—to replace dozens of mongrel, unknown, unacknowledged makers of a fabric, a dress essential, a food, with a standard trade-marked brand, backed by the national advertising that in itself has come to be a guarantee of worth with the public.

But advertising came early to do more than imprint a brand name on the public consciousness. It had to entice consumers to buy, and in so doing it dangled before them the promise of a better life through consumer goods. "How many advertisers," asked Walter Dill Scott in a remarkably perceptive 1903 article, "describe a piano so vividly that the reader can hear it? How many food products are so described that the reader can taste the food? ... How many describe an undergarment so that the reader can feel the pleasant contact with his body? Many advertisers ... make no attempt at such a description."

But they learned quickly. Although the consumer economy did not come to full flower until the 1920s, it grew rapidly after 1900. Every large city had its magnificent emporiums like Wanamaker's or Macy's as well as more specialized retail havens. Before there were malls, there were arcades—long rows of shops on several levels in the heart of the city, enclosed by a magnificent structure of wrought iron and glass. Providence, Rhode Island, built one as early as 1828, and other cities followed with larger, more elaborate versions. Shopping itself, a pleasure once reserved for the well-to-do, became as much a national pastime as baseball or complaining about Congress.

A new life-style was emerging in the cities, fed by the growth of the middle class, a rising standard of living, new building technologies, and improved transportation. It revolved increasingly around what a later generation would call "leisure time," a term that would have drawn blank stares from Americans of an earlier era. Time away from work—and there was more of it than ever before—was devoted to pursuits that were more secular, organized, and expensive. Whole industries arose to serve leisure activities, ranging from amusement parks to professional sports to motion pictures to sporting goods to hobby shops to fashion.

The Third America was nothing less than the dawn of the most impressive material civilization yet known to the world. The speed with which worldly delights challenged and replaced more traditional values and institutions alarmed some observers. In the consumer economy, for example, the old savings ethic ("a penny saved is a penny earned") gave way of necessity to a spending ethic. Henry Ford, whose genius put the nation on wheels by applying the techniques of continuous-process production to the manufacture of automobiles, reflected this change in two of his advertisements. "Buy a Ford, Save the Difference," read his pitch in 1919. Four years later the emphasis had switched to "Buy a Ford, Spend the Difference."

This trend alarmed some religious leaders. "Some people are purchasing machines," grumbled one Chicago Baptist editor in 1909, "who might better be paying their debts." The same editor expressed a common complaint that the new machines were one more intrusion into the once inviolate Sabbath day. "They have a right to joy and gladness, to recreation and amusements," he conceded. "But...no right to forget the house of God; no right to turn the Lord's day into a day for merrymaking."

A nation that once balked even at running trains on Sunday now cheerfully devoted the day to picnics in the country or playing golf or enjoying the delights of an amusement park or watching the local baseball team play. The "good life" came to be dominated less by piety or the consolations of religion than by material goods and earthly pleasures. But there were subtle traps here as well. Once people acquired more material goods, they became less satisfied with what they had and wanted still more. As the standard of living rose, so did both the expectations and frustrations of those who did not get what they wanted and had even come to expect as their due. In the consumer economy today's luxuries became tomorrow's necessities.

Here was a problem of moral philosophy that baffled a people who had once excelled at moral philosophy but were fast losing their interest in it. Underlying social tensions were shoved aside with the blithe promise that sooner or later everyone would get his piece of the economic pie because it would always be large enough to feed a nation of growing appetites. Only when depressions and recessions wracked the economy periodically did these questions burst forth more insistently. Even then the solutions were nearly always defined as larger pieces of the pie on the assumption that the pie would always grow faster than the appetites seeking shares of it.

The American experience in World War I extended this pattern and set the stage for a new era of expansion, much as the Civil War had done earlier. These two generations lay on opposite sides of cataclysmic wars that reshaped their worlds. The secession of the South in 1860–1861 had removed from Congress the largest bloc of opponents to policies needed to spur industrial growth. During that war Congress passed a stream of legislation that shaped the era of postwar expansion.

World War I exerted a similar effect but on a global scale. In 1914 the United States already led the world in manufacturing with 56 percent of total output compared with 16 percent for Germany and 14 percent for Great Britain. But it owed investors in other countries $3.8 billion, which meant that interest on that amount flowed overseas. By 1919 the war had made the United States a creditor to foreign nations by $12.5 billion, thereby turning what had been debt service into income. The United States emerged from the war as the economic giant of the world by default. While its industrial and agricultural might grew, other nations lay exhausted and shattered by their long and desperate struggle.

The war boosted the American economy in other ways. It spurred a trend toward standardization in industry. To simplify production, for example, the varieties of steel plows were reduced from 312 to 76, of planters and drills from 784 to 29, of automobile tires from 287 to 3. Wartime demand relieved the economy of a nagging recession that had plagued it since 1913. It created jobs and sent people streaming into industrial cities. Within a year after the Remington Arms Company built a new factory in Bridgeport, Connecticut, the town's population soared from 115,000 to 165,000.

During six months in 1917 more than 600,000 blacks (and even more Southern whites) migrated to Northern cities in search of work. Their quest for a better life marked the first major shift in the nation's traditional racial demography. The presence of large black populations in cities not accustomed to them provoked outbursts of bigotry, Northern style, that culminated in a series of bloody race riots. A growing wave of intolerance spawned in large part by the war erupted periodically into violence against other groups as well as blacks.

Older industries profited from wartime demands, and new industries shot into prominence. When the United States entered the conflict, products once obtained from Germany, such as dyes, medicines, industrial solvents, and chemicals, had to be made by American firms. Their task was made easier in some cases by confiscating German patents. During the war American production of coal-tar chemicals soared from $13.5 million to $133.5 million, that of drugs from $177 million to $418 million. Long-suffering farmers saw crop prices jump as they had not in decades; farm income doubled between 1914 and 1918. Cotton, which had brought 12 cents a pound in 1914, fetched 34 cents in 1920, and wheat jumped from 94 cents to $2.46 a bushel.

The war effort also cleansed the tarnished reputation of businessmen and reversed the trend toward more regulation that had characterized the Progressive years. This was inevitable, if only because giant corporations were in the best position to fill large orders for military equipment. Businessmen were also needed in Washington to help organize and administer the war effort, which required the kind of experience possessed by the managers of giant corporations. Their presence and influence helped strengthen ties between government and business that had weakened in recent years.

After 1920 three Republican presidents would preside over a decade of prosperity that confirmed the triumph of the consumer economy. During their reign the flowering of the Third America gave way to the unabashed materialism of the Fourth America, in which earlier trends accelerated at an astonishing rate. This saga would have an abrupt and unhappy ending in the form of the Great Depression. It also started unhappily with a severe recession in 1919–1921 as the economy, having been mobilized for war production, struggled to convert to peacetime needs.

As this recession showed, the war was not an unmixed blessing. It took Americans on an economic roller-coaster ride that proved to be a preview of the century to come. The economy was wallowing in recession when war broke out in Europe. As orders for war materials from the Allies poured into American plants, a lukewarm economy rapidly heated up. United States Steel, which had struggled to pay its bills in 1913, found itself swamped with a backlog of orders by the end of 1915 as more than a third of its output went overseas. Pig iron production doubled in a year, and the large shipments of American grain heading abroad brought a flurry of orders for farm machinery. Exports leaped from $2.3 billion in 1914 to $6.2 billion in 1917.

Prosperity helped reelect Woodrow Wilson in 1916, but the surging economy soon began to produce shortages and with them the scourge of inflation. Once the United States entered the war in April 1917, these pressures intensified. To make mobilization as efficient as possible, the War Industries Board was created and given broad powers over the economy. Drastic measures were imposed to expedite the war effort; when the railroad system found itself gridlocked during 1917, Wilson nationalized the roads and placed them under a new government agency.

Overheated by wartime demands, the economy faced a menace it had not known in decades: runaway inflation. Labor shortages, spurred by rising demand on one side and the abrupt end to immigration caused by the war on the other, drove manufacturing wages up from an average of $580 per year in 1914 to $980 in 1918 and $1,358 in 1920. But consumer prices doubled between 1914 and 1920, and wholesale prices jumped 126 percent, swallowing up most of these gains and imposing severe hardships on those whose pay rose little if at all. Land values rose as farmers, basking in prices they had not seen in years, raised the nation's total farm mortgage debt from $4.7 million in 1914 to $8.4 million in 1920.

Then came the armistice in November 1918, and the roller coaster plunged abruptly downward. Government agencies halted overtime work for employees and canceled $2.5 billion in outstanding contracts at a time when a quarter of the civilian labor force was employed in making wartime goods. Within six months two million servicemen were discharged and thrown onto the job market of a contracting economy; another two million soon followed. Factories that had been running at capacity found their orders withering away, and demand for farm products dropped almost as quickly. Price and other controls were removed as the elaborate system of government agencies created to run the war were dismantled with almost indecent haste.

The year that followed tested the resolve of Americans as much as the war had. The economy was out of joint and had to retool itself for peacetime. Meanwhile, inflation ravaged dwindling incomes, and even giant corporations found their vaunted efficiency tested severely by the sudden halt in orders that produced bloated inventories. Julius Rosenwald of Sears kept that giant firm from defaulting on payments to suppliers by dipping into his personal fortune. The Armour family was not so fortunate; the losses suffered by their meat company cost them control of the firm. Henry Ford staved off disaster by forcing his dealers to buy cars they had no chance of selling. General Motors simply bit the bullet and wrote off $83 million in inventory losses for 1921 and 1922.

Society was no less out of joint than the economy. The war effort had fanned hatred for the enemy and intolerances that could not be turned off like a spigot on Armistice Day. A new ogre, the Russian Revolution, had sprung up during the war and alarmed Americans with the specter of communism spreading into the vacuum of postwar Europe. Americans feared and despised communism because it targeted three of their most cherished maxims: private property, religion, and the open system free of government controls. These fears triggered a wave of mass hysteria in 1919 known as the Red Scare, which directed its wrath mostly at immigrants and radicals. The scare thrust into prominence an ambitious young bureaucrat named J. Edgar Hoover and cast an ugly pall of intolerance across the coming decade.

Racial tensions continued to grip American cities throughout 1919. The corpse of the Ku Klux Klan sprang back to life, broadening its message of hate beyond blacks to Jews, immigrants, radicals, and anything it deemed as not "100 percent American." Women, who had moved into the work force during the war, resented being pushed back out as the troops returned home. The women's suffrage movement was at last nearing its goal of winning the right to vote. If this were not enough, Prohibition had also gained approval at long last and was about to be imposed on a reluctant populace.

Nothing seemed right with the world in 1920. The greatest war in human history had sent an entire world order and epoch of history crashing into flames with losses of life so huge as to defy comprehension. On its heels had come the worst pandemic in modern history, the flu epidemic of 1918–1919 which killed more than 21 million people worldwide and 675,000 Americans in only a few months. The economy was a mess, society in turmoil, perhaps civilization itself on the verge of collapse. A new generation of Americans, emerging from the rubble, heaped bitter denunciations on the smug façade of Victorian culture and repudiated everything it stood for.

It seemed as if the Third America had flowered and faded in the war and its aftermath. Yet with astonishing resilience this cluster of problems gave way to a buoyant era that ushered in the Fourth America over which the consumer economy would rule. The war had closed the door on one epoch and set the stage for another, leaving as its legacy the same roller-coaster pattern that had characterized the economy through those turbulent wartime years.

# Epilogue: The United States in 1920

Two souls dwell in the bosom ... of the American people. The one loves the Abundant Life, as expressed in the cheap and plentiful products of a large-scale mass production and distribution.... The other soul yearns for former simplicities, for decentralization, for the interests of the "little man," revolts against high-pressure salesmanship, denounces "monopoly" and "economic empires," and seeks means of breaking them up.

—Dorothy Thompson,
*New York Herald Tribune* (1938)

No ONE COULD ignore the black cloud that hung ominously over the World Series of 1920. During the last month of the regular season, amid a torrid pennant race, baseball fans were stunned by reports that the 1919 Series had been fixed. Eight members of the Chicago White Sox were charged with conspiring with gamblers to throw games. Although a jury acquitted all of them, newly appointed Commissioner of Baseball Judge Kenesaw Mountain Landis did not even wait for the verdict before banning all eight players from baseball for life.

They have been stigmatized ever since as the Black Sox, and the scandal threatened the future of major league baseball. After the last game of the 1919 Series, writer Hugh Fullerton, suspicious of what he had seen, predicted that "Yesterday's game in all probability is the last that ever will be played in any World Series." He was wrong, and the players did their best in 1920 to prove him wrong. During the season Babe Ruth, who had been sold to the New York Yankees by the Boston Red Sox, electrified fans by belting an astounding fifty-four home runs, far above the record-setting twenty-nine he had hit the season before. Only three years earlier Wally Pipp of the Yankees had led the league with nine home runs.

The World Series topped even Ruth's feat. In the fifth game Cleveland's Elmer Smith hit the first grand slam homer ever in the Series only to be upstaged by teammate Bill Wambsganss, who pulled off the first unassisted triple play as the Indians beat the Brooklyn Dodgers. The largest crowd to witness one of the games was 27,525, a far cry from the 2,700 who saw the first Series game in 1882 though not that far from the 18,801 fans who attended the third game of the first modern World Series in 1903. The rest of the country had to follow the action by newspaper, but something new had appeared on the horizon that would soon dramatically change sports and most other aspects of American life. In 1920 the first broadcast radio station went on the air in Pittsburgh.

Baseball was not the only sport that attracted wide public attention. Ethelda M. Bleibtrey thrilled Americans by capturing three swimming medals at the Olympics in Antwerp. Harvard edged Oregon 7–6 in the Rose Bowl. Big Bill Tilden swept the tennis championship at Wimbledon, opening a five-year reign over the sport. The American Professional Football Association was formed as eleven teams paid $100 each for a franchise. One of them, the Decatur Staleys, was represented by a baseball player named George Halas, who moved the team upstate to Chicago two years later and called them the Bears. The league itself realigned under a new title, the National Football League. Man O'War, one of the greatest race horses ever, retired to stud after winning twenty of twenty-one races.

The growing obsession for sports that seemed to grip the Fourth America revealed much about the changes that had taken place since 1850. It was partly a search for heroes, and a new kind of hero at that. The heroes of the first and second Americas had been political figures: the Founding Fathers and great national leaders like Jackson, Clay, Calhoun, and Webster. The Third America plucked its heroes from the ranks of business, the titans who fashioned the industrial miracle. The Fourth America found its heroes in fields that had scarcely existed earlier: entertainment and sports, leisure activities in a society that could afford leisure time and had created several thriving industries to serve it.

This change in types of national heroes indicated how much American life had changed in less than a century. To Americans of 1920 the world of 1850 seemed as remote as the Middle Ages. For that matter, citizens of 1850 would not have recognized much of the world of 1920—its people, machines, cities, or ways of life. In that time the population had grown 456 percent to 105.7 million and become infinitely more varied. The number of urban places had risen from 236 to 2,722, and 51 percent of the population lived in such places compared with only 15 percent in 1850. The lone city boasting more than 100,000 people in 1850 had been joined by sixty-seven others.

The industrial system that was just beginning to spread in 1850 had become a behemoth by 1920. Railroad mileage soared from 9,021 to 259,941, and tracks reached into every corner of the nation. Coal production topped 676 million tons compared with 8.3 million tons in 1850, and petroleum output reached 443 million barrels. Pig iron production jumped from 563,000 tons to 35.7 million tons. Estimates of total horsepower used exceeded 453 million, dwarfing the 8.5 million used in 1850. Of that amount, 280 million was consumed by motor vehicles, of which there were nearly 8.9

million licensed in 1920. Some 8.5 million Americans worked in factories compared with only 957,000 in 1850; the number of gainful nonfarm workers leaped from 2.8 million to 31 million. The 824 banks of 1850 had become 30,909 in 1920. Inventors took out 37,798 patents compared with 883 in 1850.

Although the population mushroomed, families grew smaller. The birth rate per thousand dropped from 43.3 to 27.7, and the average household of 5.55 in 1850 shrank to 4.34 in 1920. School enrollments per 100 rose from 56.2 to 65.7 for whites, and soared from a paltry 1.8 to 53.5 for black Americans. One American family in three had a car and/or a telephone, but only about one in ten urban homes and hardly any rural ones were wired for electricity. The nation boasted 2,441 newspapers compared with 254 in 1850, and 52,641 post offices instead of 18,417. More people voted in elections, but the proportion of those voting in the presidential election shrank alarmingly from nearly 73 percent in 1848 to 49 percent in 1920. Had more information made people less interested in politics, or had more distractions like sports simply bumped politics from the center stage it had long occupied in American life?

Government grew much larger, though nothing like what it would become in the Fourth America. The 26,274 federal workers of 1851 increased to 655,265 in 1920, and federal expenditures rose from $39.5 million to nearly $6.36 billion. The national debt, a modest $63.5 million in 1850, pushed $24.3 billion in 1920 and cost every citizen $228.23 in interest compared with $2.85 in 1850. Although the armed forces reduced their strength quickly after the war, the military still had 343,302 people on active duty compared with 20,824 in 1850.

These figures depict a striking change in the dimensions of American life but only hint at even more startling changes in its texture. Where were bloomers and corsets, buggies and blacksmiths, parlors and the pianos around which family and friends gathered to sing? These elements and the way of life attached to them still existed, mostly in small towns, but with not as many people in as many ways or as many towns. They were fast becoming a sort of national still life, the shards and icons of a vanishing way of life that would later be fast frozen in *Our Town*, a 1938 play by Thornton Wilder that remains immensely popular for its poignant view of small-town New England.

Life in the Fourth America was faster, louder, more complex, and more distracting. New technologies were largely responsible for these changes. Two of them, the automobile and electricity, were already making their influence felt and would soon revamp almost every aspect of American life and society. The motor car was no longer a plaything for the rich thanks to Henry Ford, who made one of every two cars sold in 1920.

Another new technology, the motion picture, had already gained immense popularity as a form of entertainment and become a major industry. Films exerted a profound effect on American life, opening windows of experience to ordinary people who saw for the first time images of people, places, clothes, and customs they would otherwise never have seen. Movies spawned their own cults of heroes or "stars," and did much to trigger a growing phenomenon in the consumer economy: the fad. Other machines enabled people to hear in their own homes music performed by great artists they might otherwise never hear or see. Still another new technology gave a broad hint of future promise: 1920 witnessed the first transcontinental delivery of mail from New York to San Francisco by airplane.

These new technologies were fast broadening the gap between city and country life into a chasm. The rhythms of sun and season had given way to the inexorable beat of the clock. Nature was something found in parks or somewhere outside of town, where it could be enjoyed on an outing by car. Workers wrestled less with the elements than with the intricate coils of a bureaucracy, as far more people worked for someone else than for themselves. At home many of them enjoyed such creature comforts as running water, indoor plumbing, central heating, gas stoves, electricity, and a growing list of appliances and prepared foods.

Society had become more diffuse and fragmented as it grew more urbanized. The familiarity of small-town life gave way to the anonymity of urban life in which people lived closer to one another but often did not even know their neighbors. Activities that had once taken place in the home moved increasingly to clubs, schools, movie houses, gyms, restaurants, and elsewhere. Families that had once done most things together pursued activities that took them in different directions and often brought them back together only at mealtime. The automobile revolutionized not only leisure time but courtship as well, enabling young people to escape the watchful eye of chaperones and to broaden their range of prospects and pleasures.

The automobile also changed *where* people lived, enabling more families to move into suburbs where most families belonged to the same economic group, even though they were strangers to each other when they arrived. In these fast-growing communities on the fringes of every city, the consumer economy loomed ever larger as the unifying strand of experience among the residents. So did the emerging national culture, with its standardizing tastes and shared experiences of films, sports events, foods, clothing, clubs, books, magazines, and brand names.

Literature and the arts reflected not only this jarring change of cultural tastes but a culture in which voices from past and present vied for attention, much like the two village bands playing different tunes as they marched into the same town from opposite directions that Charles Ives depicted in his musical portrait of "Three Places in New England." Ives was the quintessential American artist—a composer of breathtaking audacity and genius who was in real life an insurance man. The best of his music had already been written well before 1920, but little of it had been heard and less of it had been understood except by some other composers.

Competing voices, many of them dissonant, filled American culture in 1920. Literature's grand old man, William Dean Howells, who championed realism and some of the past generation's finest writers, died that year. George Ade, who had amused Americans with his use of vernacular language and his portrayal of country life, published a new book called *Hand-Made Fables* that seemed an echo of yesteryear. So did Edith Wharton's masterful portrait of upper-class life, *The Age of Innocence*, which served as a requiem to another vanishing way of life. Two new voices announced their presence in 1920 by capturing different aspects of the emerging consumer society in a way that made them darlings of the new era. Sinclair Lewis trained an unblinking eye on the crass hypocrisy of small-town society in *Main Street*, while F. Scott Fitzgerald introduced Americans to the wit and glamour of what would become known as the "Smart Set" in *This Side of Paradise*.

Andrew Carnegie's autobiography also appeared in 1920. The saga of his "rags-to-riches" climb to wealth and power still served as a prototype of the American Dream for those who aspired to great achievements. But Carnegie, who had died the year before, had ceased to be the role model for most Americans. The day of the great entrepreneur had given way to the age of the salesman and the belief that the man (for business was still a man's world) who could sell *himself* could sell anything to anybody. The Carnegie most read by Americans of the next generation would not be Andrew but Dale, whose best-selling *How to Win Friends and Influence People* appeared in 1937.

A commanding new voice in American theatre, Eugene O'Neill, announced his presence in 1920 with two brilliant and startlingly different plays, *Beyond the Horizon*, which won the Pulitzer Prize, and *The Emperor Jones*. But far fewer people saw O'Neill's work than watched Mary Pickford in the hit movie *Pollyanna*. And while Charles Ives's complex but fiercely American music remained unknown, audiences at home and abroad flocked eagerly to hear the ever evolving varieties of that unique form of American music called jazz. In 1920 Paul Whiteman, one of the best-known band leaders, took his group on a triumphal tour of Europe.

Technology challenged old forms of art and created new ones. Books and theatre had to compete with film, painting with photography. The arts groped painfully toward new forms of expression that distanced them still more from traditional culture. In painting, naturalism gave way to modernism, which rejected the old imitation of nature and tried to penetrate beneath the surface of things to inner meanings through the use of bold and unfamiliar techniques. As art grew more abstract it became more abstruse to the layman, driving a wedge between the artist and his audience and between the audience and its culture.

The war had shown Americans that technology could be lethal as well as benign. This pattern of mixed blessings continued in 1920 when Harvey Cushing excited surgeons by developing new techniques in brain surgery and retired officer John T. Thompson patented his deadly submachine or "Tommy" gun, thereby giving brain surgeons more business while placing a potent new weapon in the hands of a new breed of criminal who would arise to mock the good intentions of Prohibition: the mobster.

The flood of immigration that had given the Third America so much of its character slowed to a trickle, marking the end of an era. War first slammed the gates shut in 1914, but the United States left them closed afterward. Social turmoil at home made Americans suspicious of and hostile to foreigners. The hatreds and hysteria unleashed by war were fanned by the Bolshevik Revolution raging in Russia and threatening to overspread the rest of Europe.

During 1919 the outburst of public hysteria directed at communism targeted foreign radicals as its obvious agents. Before the Red Scare had run its sordid course, thousands of innocent, bewildered immigrants had been detained and several hundred of them sent to Russia on ships derisively called "Soviet Arks." During these turbulent months thousands of American workers went on strike seeking wage hikes to meet the rampant inflation. In many cases opportunistic business leaders broke the strikes by denouncing them as communist inspired and led.

The Red Scare withered away as abruptly as it had come, but its aftermath lingered in 1920. One September day at noontime a bomb blast shattered the bustle of Wall Street outside the offices of J. P. Morgan & Company, killing thirty people and wounding three hundred more (of whom ten died later). No clue to the identity of the bomber was ever found. In May two Italian anarchists, Nicola Sacco and Bartolomeo Vanzetti, were arrested and charged with murdering a paymaster and guard at a shoe factory in South Braintree, Massachusetts. Their case gained national attention because of its complexity and the belief that their political views had more to do with their conviction than the case brought by the prosecution. Despite widespread protest and fresh evidence, both men were electrocuted in August 1927.

The Sacco-Vanzetti saga reflected a curious paradox in the United States of 1920: it had become a nation filled with more differences than ever before, yet its people seemed more fearful of differences than ever before. Apart from its own cultural pluralism, the country found itself thrust to the center of the world stage for the first time. For half a century the United States had been marching toward world economic supremacy. In 1920 she formally assumed the throne in a world ravaged by war and influenza.

Half a century earlier, Americans were busy healing the deep wounds of a civil war that had killed more of them than all the nation's wars before or since put together. In 1920 they found themselves recovering from another great war, this one on a global scale. Where the Civil War had defined once and for all American nationalism, World War I defined for the United States a new and primary role in world affairs. It was a role many Americans regarded with profound uneasiness and distaste. More than once in the coming years they would try to reject or escape from it, but in vain.

For the rest of the century the debate over the nation's proper role in world affairs would divide its people deeply. The issue that crystallized national sentiment on the subject was the long and clangorous fight over whether the United States should join the new League of Nations, an international body created in large part by the influence of our own president, Woodrow Wilson. In the end Americans rejected the League, leaving Wilson a broken, embittered man and setting themselves apart from a world in tatters.

The election of 1920 wrote the epitaph to Wilson's dream of an international order to keep the peace. Democrat James M. Cox defended the League and went down to a crushing defeat at the hands of Warren G. Harding, a handsome, charming man whose mind was an empty closet that received whatever his friends chose to hang there. Harding had stumped for a "return to normalcy," a word he had coined as one of many malaprops, and the image of restoring the good old days appealed strongly to Americans wearied by war, a failed crusade for democracy, the flu epidemic, social turmoil, and postwar recession.

Normalcy won the election and Harding was the perfect figurehead for it, but normalcy was not to be had in the world of 1920—at least not on the old terms. That world was forever gone, swept away as surely as the Old South had been by the Civil War. In its wake came first the trauma of postwar recession and dislocation. During 1920–1921, as the economy struggled to convert to peacetime production, the gross national product dipped from $40.1 billion to $37.6 billion, stocks dropped nearly 25 percent, the ranks of unemployed swelled to 4 million, half a million farmers lost their homesteads, and 100,000 businesses went bankrupt.

Ahead lay another roller-coaster era of prosperity, depression, and war, the Fourth America that would make the past seem more remote than ever before—not so much in time as in distance. Technology turned the world over faster every time around, it seemed, and the more things changed, the more Americans padded themselves with nostalgia. Harding's call for normalcy appealed to this nostalgia, which during the 1920s would find expression in political, social, and religious movements such as fundamentalism, "hundred percentism," and a revolt against modernism.

Dorothy Thompson's observation in 1938 was right on target. The nostalgia Americans felt for an earlier, simpler world did not apply to what was in that world so much as the fact that it was simpler. Without realizing it they were caught up in the paradox of progress, in which they both repudiated the Victorian world and its values while longing for its simpler, more settled pace of life in which everyone and everything had a clearly defined place. But in their hearts they had no desire to return to it because the modern world, with all its complexity and confusion, had opened to them new vistas of material prosperity, creature comforts, and pleasures of which they had never dreamed.

Late in the 1880s that perceptive Englishman, Lord James Bryce, had observed that life in America was "that of the squirrel in his revolving cage, never still even when it does not seem to change.... It is unusually hard for any one to withdraw his mind from the endless variety of external impressions and interests which daily life presents, and which impinge upon the mind." By 1920 the wheel was revolving ever faster, and the sensations pouring in on the average American had multiplied to an extent that Bryce could not have conceived.

The productive miracles of the Third America had launched the American people into a brave new world of material civilization. Where it would lead they had no way of knowing, but of one thing they could be certain: whatever their destination, they would get there faster than anyone had ever gone anywhere before them.

# A Note on Sources

THIS BOOK HAS drawn on a wide variety of sources, only some of which can be noted here. The works mentioned here are relevant to most if not all the chapters. Two books essential to grasping the entire period are Alfred D. Chandler, Jr.'s monumental *The Visible Hand* (Cambridge, Mass., 1977) and David Potter's seminal *People of Plenty* (Chicago, 1954). For an overview of manufacturing see David A. Hounshell, *From the American System to Mass Production, 1800–1932: The Development of Manufacturing Technology in the United States* (Baltimore, 1984). See also Robert Wiebe, *The Search for Order, 1877–1920* (New York, 1967) and Maury Klein and Harvey A. Kantor, *Prisoners of Progress: American Industrial Cities, 1850–1920 (New York, 1976).*

### 1. THE INDUSTRIALIZING OF AMERICA

The factors of industrialization are discussed in more detail in Klein and Kantor, *Prisoners of Progress.* Chandler's key article on the importance of anthracite coal can be found in Thomas K. McCraw, ed., *The Essential Alfred Chandler* (Cambridge, Mass., 1988). For Eli Whitney see Constance Green, *Eli Whitney and the Birth of American Technology* (Boston, 1956). The role of railroads is discussed in Chandler, *The Visible Hand,* and in Albro Martin, *Railroads Triumphant* (New York, 1992). On the telegraph see Robert L. Thompson, *Wiring a Continent* (Princeton, 1947). More detail on the role of markets can be found in Karl Polanyi, *The Great Transformation* (Boston, 1944).

## 2. THE NEW ENTREPRENEURS

The role of American entrepreneurs, with profiles of several key figures, can be found in Jonathan R. T. Hughes, *The Vital Few* (New York, 1986); Harold C. Livesay, *American Made* (Boston, 1979); and Gerald Gunderson, *The Wealth Makers* (New York, 1990). See also Peter Drucker, *Innovation and Entrepreneurship* (New York, 1985). The seminal figure in entrepreneurial theory is Joseph Schumpeter; see his *The Theory of Economic Development* (New York, 1934) and *Capitalism, Socialism, and Democracy* (New York, 1937). For the role of law see J. Willard Hurst's insightful *Law and the Conditions of Freedom in the Nineteenth-Century United States* (Madison, Wisc., 1956). No student of American history should miss Alexis de Tocqueville, *Democracy in America*, 2 vols. (New York, 1835). More detail on the entrepreneurs coming of age during the Civil War is in Maury Klein, "The Boys Who Stayed Behind: Northern Industrialists and the Civil War," in James I. Robertson, Jr., and Richard M. McMurry, eds., *Rank and File: Civil War Essays in Honor of Bell Irvin Wiley* (San Rafael, Calif., 1976).

## 3. THE CORPORATE ECONOMY

For theoretical background see Kenneth E. Boulding, *The Organizational Revolution* (Chicago, 1953). An old warhorse, Arthur S. Dewing, *The Financial Policy of Corporations*, 2 vols. (New York, 1953), is still useful as an introduction to the basic elements of corporations. Alfred D. Chandler, Jr., *Strategy and Structure* (Cambridge, Mass., 1962) provides case studies of Standard Oil and Sears, Roebuck. See also Richard S. Tedlow, *New and Improved: The Story of Mass Marketing in America* (New York, 1990). Details on the merger movement can be found in Ralph L. Nelson, *Merger Movements in American Industry, 1895–1956* (Princeton, 1959), and in Naomi R. Lamoreaux, *The Great Merger Movement in American Business, 1895–1904* (New York, 1985).

## 4. THE BUSINESS OF FARMING

For a brief, incisive history of American farming see John T. Schlebecker, *Whereby We Thrive: A History of American Farming, 1607–1972* (Ames, Ia., 1975). Fred A. Shannon, *The Farmer's Last Frontier: Agriculture, 1860–1897* (New York, 1945), is a somewhat dated but still informative classic. John G. Clark, *The Grain Trade in the Old Northwest* (Urbana, Ill., 1966), is filled with information on that subject. Harold D. Woodman, *King Cotton and His Retainers: Financing and Marketing the Cotton Crop of the South, 1800–1925* (Lexington, Ky., 1968), details the changes in the handling of that crop.

## 5. THE CORPORATE SOCIETY

Henry George, *Progress and Poverty* (New York, 1879), is invaluable for capturing the spirit of the age, as are Henry Demarest Lloyd, *Wealth Against Commonwealth* (New York, 1894); Herbert Croly, *The Promise of American Life* (New York, 1909); Walter Rauschenbusch, *Christianity and the Social Crisis* (New York, 1907); and Walter Weyl, *The New Democracy* (New York, 1912). Josiah Strong, *Our Country* (New York, 1885), and Madison Grant, *The Passing of the Great Race* (New York, 1916), articulate the nativist reaction, details on which can be found in John Higham, *Strangers in the Land* (New Brunswick, N.J., 1955). For an overview of the immigrant experience see Roger Daniels, *Coming to America* (New York, 1990). Carl Wittke, *We Who Built America* (New York, 1939), is still useful. See also Philip Taylor, *The Distant Magnet* (New York, 1971), and David

Ward, *Cities and Immigrants* (New York, 1971). For the rise of the labor movement see Melvyn Dubofsky, *Industrialism and the American Worker, 1865–1920* (Arlington Heights, Ill., 1985), which has a full bibliography. Joseph Rayback, *A History of American Labor* (New York, 1966), is a standard summary. See also Herbert G. Gutman, *Work, Culture, and Society in Industrializing America* (New York, 1976), and James R. Green, *The World of the Worker* (New York, 1980). David Montgomery, *The Fall of the House of Labor* (New York, 1987), offers a new interpretation. Daniel Nelson, *Managers and Workers: The Origins of the New Factory System in the United States, 1880–1920* (Madison, Wisc., 1975), covers that important subject well. Useful insights on a variety of subjects can be found in Olivier Zunz, *Making America Corporate* (Chicago, 1990). Morton Keller, *Affairs of State: Public Life in Late Nineteenth Century America* (Cambridge, Mass., 1977), contains useful information on state and local governments during that period. Harold Zink, *City Bosses in the United States* (Durham, N.C., 1930), remains a useful collective portrait.

### 6. The New American Landscape

Useful works on the rise of the city include Adna F. Weber, *The Growth of Cities in the Nineteenth Century* (New York, 1899); Arthur M. Schlesinger, *The Rise of the City* (New York, 1933); Sam Bass Warner, Jr., *The Urban Wilderness* (New York, 1972); and Blake McKelvey, *The Urbanization of America, 1860–1915* (New Brunswick, N.J., 1963). The classic study of the middle class is C. Wright Mills, *White Collar* (New York, 1951). See also Lewis Corey, "Problems of the Peace: IV. The Middle Class," *Antioch Review* (March 1945), and Stuart M. Blumin, *The Emergence of the Middle Class* (New York, 1989). Burton J. Bledstein, *The Culture of*

Professionalism (New York, 1976), is informative and provocative on that subject. Detail on the accounting profession can be found in Stephen A. Zeff, ed., *The U.S. Accounting Profession in the 1890s and Early 1900s* (New York, 1988). The Sears saga is detailed in Boris Emmet and John E. Jeuck, *Catalogues and Counters: A History of Sears, Roebuck and Company* (Chicago, 1950).

### 7. TECHNOLOGY TRIUMPHANT

The most insightful study of technology in this period is Thomas P. Hughes, *American Genesis* (New York, 1989). John W. Oliver, *History of American Technology* (New York, 1956), is useful but prosaic; see also Bruce Norman, *The Inventing of America* (New York, 1976). David F. Noble, *America by Design: Science, Technology, and the Rise of Corporate Capitalism* (New York, 1977); Samuel Haber, *Efficiency and Uplift* (Chicago, 1964); and Brooke Hindle, *Emulation and Invention* (New York, 1982), offer valuable insights. Edward W. Byrn, *The Progress of Invention* (New York, 1900), is invaluable for capturing the state of the art at the turn of the century along with the attitude of reverence toward technology. Changes in energy use are detailed in Sam H. Schurr, et al, *Energy in the American Economy, 1850–1975* (Baltimore, 1960). Thomas P. Hughes, *Networks of Power: Electrification in Western Society, 1880–1930* (Baltimore, 1983), provides an overview of the early era of electricity. See also Harold C. Passer, *The Electrical Manufacturers, 1875–1900* (Cambridge, Mass., 1953). Matthew Josephson, *Edison* (New York, 1959), details that inventor's career. Forrest McDonald, *Insull* (Chicago, 1962), makes a persuasive case for the seminal role of Samuel Insull in the electric power industry. Victor S. Clark, *History of Manufactures in the United States*, 3 vols. (New York, 1929), is a mine of information on a variety of matters including technology. For construction technology see Carl Condit, *American Building Art* (New York, 1960) and *American Building* (Chicago, 1968). Different aspects of urban technology are treated in Nelson M. Blake, *Water for the Cities* (Syracuse, 1956); David McCullough, *The Great Bridge* (New York, 1972); and John A. Miller, *Fares Please! From Horsecars to Steamliners* (New York, 1941). The Centennial Exhibition is covered in Dee Brown, *The Year of the Century: 1876* (New York, 1966).

## 8. INTEGRATION AND ALIENATION

Irvin G. Wylie, *The Self-Made Man in America: The Myth of Rags to Riches* (New Brunswick, N.J., 1954), treats that subject in detail. The standard work on investment banking is Vincent P. Carosso, *Investment Banking in America* (Cambridge, Mass., 1970). See also Fritz Redlich, *The Molding of American Banking* (New York, 1951), and Harold van B. Cleveland and Thomas F. Huertas, *Citibank 1812–1970* (Cambridge, Mass., 1985). The classic observer of slum life was Jacob Riis; see his *How the Other Half Lives* (New York, 1890), *The Children of the Poor* (New York, 1892), and *A Ten Years' War: An Account of the Battle with the Slums* (Boston, 1900). No student should overlook Jane Addams, *Twenty Years at Hull House* (New York, 1910). See also Robert A. Woods, et al, *The Poor in Great Cities* (New York, 1895), and Robert Hunter, *Poverty* (New York, 1904). For an earlier view see Charles Loring Brace, *The Dangerous Classes of New York and Twenty Years' Work Among Them* (New York, 1872). Moses Rischin, *The Promised City: New York City's Jews, 1870–1914* (Cambridge, Mass., 1962), depicts one ethnic group's experience. For urban political machines see Lincoln Steffens, *The Shame of the Cities* (New York, 1904) and

*Autobiography* (New York, 1931). For the battle over education see Lawrence A. Cremin, *The Transformation of the
School* (New York, 1961).


## 9. THE FLOWERING OF THE THIRD AMERICA

Lord James Bryce, *The American Commonwealth*, 2 vols.
(New York, 1888), is filled with observations and insights
on American life. For differing views of regulation see
Hans B. Thorelli, *Federal Antitrust Policy* (Baltimore, 1954);
Gabriel Kolko, *Railroads and Regulation* (Princeton, 1965);
Albro Martin, *Enterprise Denied* (New York, 1971); and
Thomas K. McCraw, *Prophets of Regulation* (Cambridge,
Mass., 1984). For a short history of the Interstate Commerce
Commission see Ari and Olive Hoogenboom, *A History of
the ICC: From Panacea to Palliative* (New York, 1976).
Broader issues are discussed in James Weinstein, *The Corpo-
rate Ideal in the Liberal State, 1900–1916* (Boston, 1968). For a
comprehensive view of the relationship between the market,
the law, and politics, see Martin J. Sklar, *The Corporate
Reconstruction of American Capitalism* (New York, 1988).
Daniel Horowitz, *The Morality of Spending: Attitudes Toward the Consumer Society in America, 1875–1940* (Baltimore,
1985), provides insight into that subject. Peter Fearon, *War,
Prosperity and Depression: The U.S. Economy, 1917–1945* (Lawrence, Kans., 1987), provides a brief discussion of the transition from wartime, while Robert K. Murray, *Red Scare* (New
York, 1955), covers that topic well.


## EPILOGUE

The organizational structure of the Fourth America is
treated in Louis Galambos and Joseph Pratt, *The Rise of the*

*Corporate Commonwealth* (New York, 1988). Frederick Lewis Allen, *Only Yesterday* (New York, 1931), is a delightful and informative social history of the 1920s. On the role of the automobile see James J. Flink, *America Adopts the Automobile, 1895–1910* (Cambridge, Mass., 1970). The flu epidemic is detailed in Alfred W. Crosby, *America's Forgotten Pandemic* (New York, 1989).

# Index

# A NOTE ON THE AUTHOR

Maury Klein was born in Memphis, Tennessee, studied at Knox College, and received M.A. and Ph.D. degrees from Emory University. He is now professor of history and director of the honors program at the University of Rhode Island. Mr. Klein's books include *Prisoners of Progress: American Industrial Cities, 1850–1920* (with Harvey A. Kantor), *The Life and Legend of Jay Gould*, and a two-volume history of the Union Pacific railroad.